Richard Archbold and the Archbold Biological Station

The Archbold Biological Station Board of Trustees, November 1998: back row, left to right, Robert Lloyd George, Carter R. Leidy III, Donna Hufty Lloyd George, John Archbold Hufty, Walter C. Sedgwick, Richard B. Root; center, left to right, Frances Archbold Hufty (chair), Mary Page Hufty Alegria, Daniel S. Alegria; front row, left to right, Sebastian Atucha, Lela P. Love, Frances H. Leidy. Photo by N. Deyrup.

Richard Archbold and the Archbold Biological Station

ROGER A. MORSE

University Press of Florida

Gainesville · Tallahassee · Tampa · Boca Raton

Pensacola · Orlando · Miami · Jacksonville

05   04   03   02   01   00   6   5   4   3   2   1

LIBRARY OF CONGRESS CATALOGING-IN-PUBLICATION DATA
Morse, Roger A.
Richard Archbold and the Archbold Biological Station / Roger A. Morse
p. cm.
Includes bibliographical references and index.
ISBN 0-8130-1761-0 (cloth: alk. paper)
1. Archbold, Richard. 2. Naturalists—United States Biography.
3. Archbold Biological Station. I. Title.
QH31.A66M67 2000
508'.092—dc21 99-41986

The University Press of Florida is the scholarly publishing agency for the State
University System of Florida, comprising Florida A&M University, Florida
Atlantic University, Florida International University, Florida State University,
University of Central Florida, University of Florida, University of North Flor-
ida, University of South Florida, and University of West Florida.

University Press of Florida
15 Northwest 15th Street
Gainesville, FL 32611–2079
http://www.upf.com

Contents

Foreword

Writing this foreword at my desk in the director's office at Archbold Biological Station, I look out over one of the most scientifically interesting and threatened ecosystems in the world, the Florida scrub. To understand why Archbold Biological Station is here, one has to know the events and circumstances that prescribed the course of the life of one man, Richard Archbold. Although he rarely wrote of himself, knowledge about Richard Archbold still abounds—personal acquaintances, press clippings, archives at the American Museum of Natural History, and records at Archbold Biological Station. Roger Morse has filled the void in this biography, weaving much of the available information into a cohesive history of the man. He navigates us through Richard Archbold's early endeavors with the American Museum of Natural History, the headline years of his expedition era, and the establishment of Archbold Biological Station. Although this biography concludes with his death in 1976, his lifetime endeavors live on at the station. It is almost overwhelming to recognize the extent to which the modern station, nearly a quarter of a century later, has carried his life's vision forward.

Richard Archbold had a sense of what he wanted to achieve for the station from the outset. In 1944, just after he had moved to Central Florida, he and his scientific advisory board asked Leonard Brass, a colleague from the expedition eras and resident scientist at the station, to write an article for *Science* to explain the purpose of the newly established Archbold Biological Station. Brass wrote that "probably no other locality, and certainly no other established station in southern Florida, offers such a variety of interest for zoological, botanical and ecological research." With a huge expansion in station facilities and the ever-decreasing acreage of pristine habitats in Florida, his statement is even truer today. With over 5,000 acres of globally imperiled scrub habitats, the station is acknowledged as one of the most superbly appointed field sites in North America. Today's scientific visitor sweeps down the oak-lined drive, rounds the corner, and is greeted by a group of impressive buildings, their magnificent construction endowing an ageless aura, and usually bustling with students, scientists, and visiting schoolchildren. Visiting biologists have access to laboratories specializing in ornithology, vertebrate biology, insect biology and plant ecology, a library housing hundreds of scientific publications, and complex computing facilities. The land management program, an education department, and the MacArthur Agro-ecology Research Center, a full-scale working cattle ranch focused on the relationship between agricultural practices and Florida's native biodiversity, are all part of the activities. Archbold Biological Station is a sanctuary for biologists, where they can derive inspiration and extraordinary scientific findings from the surrounding natural communities and ecological processes. Just as in Richard Archbold's day, it is a place where many of the world's greatest ecologists meet to conduct research and exchange ideas in a congenial atmosphere with like-minded colleagues.

Richard Archbold is still omnipresent at the station, in aural history, in atmosphere, in sense of purpose, and in continued family involvement. Many of those who knew him are around regularly—Glen Woolfenden, previous executive directors Jim Layne and John Fitzpatrick, as well as other visitors including Chet Winegarner, Tom Eisner, and Roger Morse. They share many stories, some memorable, describing long evenings set in motion with Johnnie Walker Black Label and filled with Archbold's tales of earlier adventures and escapades. Recalling the challenges he faced with bouts of narcolepsy, they describe moments that were sometimes amusing and at other times worrisome. They depict, by day, a shy and retiring man, generous, supportive of scientific projects and scientists, enthusiastic about all sorts of experimental equipment, and genuinely concerned about issues facing the local community.

The station's very buildings still resonate with these stories of Archbold's interests and personality, and retain much of the atmosphere of what was his home for a quarter of a century. The same furnishings are there in some cases—the large oak buffet in the dining room, faded pictures of scenes from earlier expeditions and adventures in the Florida scrub, framed awards and accolades for his contributions. Intriguing expedition artifacts, such as the huge elephant bird egg he bartered for in Madagascar, are lodged, somewhat haphazardly, rather as they would be in your own home, in nooks and crannies, and along the walls, interspersed among daily station comings and goings. This feeling of home captures his presence and creates a warm and welcoming atmosphere.

Richard Archbold's lasting gift to the station and to science, his other omnipresent contribution, is the strong and healthy endowment administered by many of his family who serve on the board of trustees. This book's final chapter, by Frances Hufty, Archbold's sister and chair of the board of trustees, is a fitting tribute to all that she and other members of his family have accomplished in carrying forward his work for the station and for science.

Archbold Biological Station continues to sustain and expand Richard Archbold's interests and enthusiasm for the Florida scrub and for science. John Jerome wrote in his 1994 Essay on the Last Great Places, titled "Scrub Beautiful Scrub," "Here is all this biology, working all these complex schemes to accommodate the geographical harshness that soil, climate, altitude and aspect have dealt it. . . . What's so beautiful about scrub, you eventually come to realize, is that it works; that it simply is." It was Archbold and his station that provided biologists the opportunities to understand how the scrub works and thus to grasp fully and to fathom the wonder and beauty of this unique ecosystem. It is a pleasure to be a part of this book and to thank Roger Morse for chronicling Richard Archbold's life, thus reminding us all why we are able to be here.

Hilary Swain,
executive director,
Archbold Biological Station

Richard Archbold, Early History

Richard Archbold (1907–76) devoted his life to the advancement of science and technology. He founded Florida's premier biological station in 1941. His special interest was mammals, but he supported other studies in biology with equal vigor. It is apparent from his unpublished, unedited, 110 pages of autobiographical notes (Archbold ca. 1939) that he especially enjoyed the outdoors and outdoor activities. Young Archbold liked the hunting he did with his father that began when he was only ten years old at the family home in southern Georgia (Thomasville).

In Georgia, Richard Archbold came under the influence of Herbert Lee Stoddard,[1] a bobwhite quail ecologist and an early advocate of controlled burns to encourage some species and discourage others. It was from Stoddard, who worked on the Archbold property and with others in the community to improve quail hunting, that Richard Archbold learned the rudiments of ecology.

As a teenager Archbold attended three private schools, which he tolerated but that did little to fire his imagination. He enjoyed the last of

John F. Archbold, son of John D. and father of Richard, who financed the American portion of the Madagascar expedition, Richard's first exploration. Station archives.

these, the Evans School in Arizona, the most—it encouraged camping, which he did frequently, often alone. Although he had no formal college education, he did spend a year as a nonregistered student at Hamilton College in upstate New York and later took classes and studied at Columbia University.

His father, John F. Archbold, recognized his son's desire to do something constructive and exciting and was easily talked into financing the U.S. share of a three-way, British, French, and American expedition to Madagascar with the stipulation that his son accompany the group. Its formal name was the Mission Zoologique Franco-Angle-Americaine, and the leader was Dr. J. Delacour representing the Museum Nationale d'Histoire Naturelle in France. The American interest in the expedition was championed by Dr. Leonard C. Sanford representing the American Museum of Natural History in New York City.[2] The expedition was in the field from April 1929 to May 1931, starting when Archbold was twenty-two years old.

The death of the American ornithologist who was to accompany the expedition led to the fortuitous meeting of Archbold and a young Cornell University graduate student, Austin L. Rand (see appendix). Rand was recommended to the expedition as a replacement ornithologist by Cornell's Professor Arthur A. Allen, a well-known ornithologist under whom Rand was studying. It is apparent from Archbold's autobiographical notes that Rand adapted well to camping and the rough living that takes place on an expedition such as that to Madagascar. The two men developed a mutual respect and remained close friends and associates the rest of their lives. Rand wrote in his tome on Madagascar birds that Archbold's "enthusiasm and energy were inspiring to those associated with him in the field."

Rand was the only member of the expedition to remain in Madagascar the whole time. His accomplishments and a record of the personnel and logistics during that time are recorded in a monumental 356-page report (Rand 1936). Rand, two years older than Archbold, had an ap-

Austin L. Rand, who, as a Cornell University graduate student, joined the Madagascar expedition and remained a close friend and confidant of Richard Archbold for the rest of his life. Station archives.

pointment through the American Museum until 1942, when World War II prevented a fourth expedition to New Guinea. However, Rand continued his association and friendship with Archbold. He owned a home near the Florida Archbold Biological Station, which he visited frequently and eventually, with his wife, occupied full-time in retirement. Rand probably had a greater influence on Archbold's career than any other person.

Richard Archbold thought for some time that he was accompanying the Madagascar expedition as a photographer. (He had developed an interest in photography as a teenager.) However, as the members of the expedition were making their plans and preparing to depart, Dr. Robert T. Hatt of the mammal department of the American Museum of Natural History asked Archbold, "Why don't you collect mammals?"[3] Hatt gave him some preliminary instructions, following which Archbold went to the family home in Georgia where he did some collecting and in the process, according to his autobiographical notes, botched the job. But he was soon shown, as he records, "how it should have been done." With those lessons and support from others of the American Museum staff, Archbold was on his way to being a full-fledged collector and preparator. He later studied mammalogy in Berlin (and elsewhere).

The Madagascar expedition was a positive experience and opened a whole new world to him. He became enthralled with the idea of biological exploration. During the 1930s he led three expeditions to New Guinea, but World War II interrupted his program. He sought to keep the expedition team together and in the process opened what he thought might be a temporary headquarters in Florida. However, the forces of war were such that while he financed several more New Guinea and New Guinea–Cape York area expeditions, he concentrated on making the Florida station into a world-class institution for biological studies.

The Madagascar Expedition

Our information concerning the French, British, and American expedition to Madagascar is found primarily in two sources: Rand's report on the birds of Madagascar (his Ph.D. thesis) (Rand 1936) and Archbold's autobiographical notes.

Rand (1936) records that a Mr. C. G. Harrold was the designated American ornithologist for the expedition but that he died just before the projected date of departure, thus delaying the group for a few weeks. It is from both of these sources that we learn about the slow way in which people were forced to travel only a few years ago. The frustrations of camp life without good transportation are also clear. Rand was kind in his words about his companions on the trip, but Archbold (1939) wrote that other than Rand and himself the others were not so well equipped for field life and ventures abroad. Admittedly, there were problems. Archbold wrote that the "land leeches were particularly potent, mosquitoes were very bad" and that one "camp was badly situated and we were never dry."

We also learn from Archbold's account the rather cruel way in which he learned about his father's death. "I came home one day to the hotel and there were three or four photographers waiting to get my picture." One of them remarked "isn't it too bad," to which Archbold replied, "I am having a wonderful time." The photographers suddenly realized that Archbold did not know about his father, but they said nothing further about it. He did not learn about his father's passing for about two weeks. However, rather than criticize these men, he offered an excuse for them, that perhaps they thought it was a false alarm. Richard Archbold was never inclined to be unkind to anyone but to give others the benefit of a doubt, that there may have been a misunderstanding.

The Madagascar expedition, especially from the American point of view, was a success. A large number of specimens was deposited in the American Museum in New York. More important, the experience gave

Archbold the knowledge he needed to prepare for future expeditions that he would lean on the rest of his career.

Archbold Family History

The source of Richard Archbold's independence and financial ability to undertake explorations was money inherited from his grandfather, John D. Archbold, through his father, John F. Archbold. To understand John D.'s success, it is best to review some family history.

The Archbolds can trace their family name back to Scotch and Irish ancestry and immigrants who entered the Americas in the 1700s. The name is on the Irish side. Their ancestry was Protestant, and they favored the Methodist faith. John Dustin Archbold, who was to become the second president of Standard Oil after John D. Rockefeller, was born in Ohio to Israel and Frances Foster Dana, both of whom started their careers as schoolteachers. When he was twenty years old, Israel attended a Methodist "protracted" meeting, a session we would today call a revival meeting, and became so enamored with religion that he became a circuit preacher. Later, when John D. was born in 1848, Israel owned a general store, though he eventually returned to the ministry and the gospel circuit. Israel and Frances had seven children, including John D., who was next to the last in age; Israel died of consumption (tuberculosis) when his young son was only ten. John D.'s mother lived until 1886, by which time he had become a major influence in the oil industry (Moore 1930).

Following Israel's death the family was destitute, and it was necessary for everyone, including John D., to work. He had no formal education beyond the Hanover (Ohio) Union School, where he apparently excelled in his studies. His grandson, Richard, the subject of this biography, wrote in his autobiographical notes that few men could add columns of figures as easily as his grandfather, though his own father, John F., was trained in the art by his father.

The first productive oil well in the United States came into being on August 27, 1859, and a new industry was under way. At the time, oil was widely considered a nuisance by the area farmers, who only thought of it as fouling the land. Some oil was skimmed off contaminated surface water and sold as a lubricant by a small number of advocates and as a medicine by others, but the quantity was small. The federal Pure Food and Drug Agency did not come into being until 1906, and the patent medicine trade and its associated quackery were the rage in the later half of the nineteenth century. Only a few years before the drilling of the first successful well others had learned to distill crude oil and to make a clear product, kerosene, which was used as an illuminate in place of more expensive beeswax candles, and whale and coal oil. It was the production of kerosene that was the basis for the Rockefeller and Archbold fortunes.

In the early part of 1864, when his desire to become a Union army drummer boy was frustrated, young John D. conferred with his mother and their Methodist minister and decided to seek his fortune in the booming oil business in Pennsylvania. At the time he left home and took the train to Titusville, Pennsylvania, the center of oil activity, he was fifteen years and ten months old. He took a variety of odd jobs but soon found regular employment with William H. Abbott, a prominent owner of oil wells, buyer of oil, president of the Citizens' Bank of Titusville, and all-around sound citizen. Abbott liked John D.'s habits and attitude, and the youth traveled with him as he made his oil-buying rounds. John D. was soon collecting bills and buying oil for his employer.

When the Abbott business was dissolved in 1869, John D. formed a partnership with H. B. Porter, who had also been an Abbott employee, and the pair bought an interest in an oil refinery. By 1872, it was the largest refinery in Titusville. In that village, John D. stayed in the American House hotel, where he met, fell in love with, and married the proprietor's daughter, Annie M. Mills. They had four children, Mary,

John D. Archbold, second president of Standard Oil after John D. Rockefeller. Station archives.

Anne, Frances, and John Foster (born May 9, 1877). John D. prospered in the oil business and in 1871 was elected secretary of the newly founded Titusville Oil Exchange, which bought, sold, and exchanged oil stocks and pipe line shares.

Competition among the oil producers, handlers, and refiners was keen and often cutthroat. John D.'s career continued to thrive, and he began to spend more time in New York City, the hub of the business world. For many years he and the Oil Exchange were in direct conflict with the interests of John D. Rockefeller and the Standard Oil Company. However, there was a major problem in the industry, overproduction, because drilling wells was so easy. John D. Rockefeller (1839–1937), nine years older than John D. Archbold, recognized the chaotic nature of the oil business and set about to combine various business interests, in effect creating a monopoly so as to eliminate the great fluctuations in oil prices. On January 10, 1870, Rockefeller and his associates formed the Standard Oil Company of Ohio with himself as the largest stockholder. In the fall of 1875, when John D. Archbold was only twenty-seven years old, he left the oil exchange and joined with the Rockefeller interests and became a director in Standard Oil.

In 1890, Rockefeller, for health reasons, began to distance himself from the Standard Oil Company, though he did not relinquish the title of president until 1911. According to Yergin (1993), he suffered from fatigue, digestive problems, and alopecia (hair loss), and by 1897 the separation was formally acknowledged. John D. Archbold, a vice president, was placed in charge and kept in weekly contact with Rockefeller, usually meeting with him on Saturday mornings. Many people did not realize a change had been made since the management system established by Rockefeller remained intact. Interestingly, it is recorded that Rockefeller regained his health by avoiding all worry, taking an abundance of exercise, and by always leaving the table a little hungry (Yergin 1993).

In 1906, the federal government initiated a suit against the Standard Oil Company, charging that the company was a monopoly and in violation of the Sherman Antitrust Law. The case went all the way to the Supreme Court, which ruled against the Standard Oil Company on May 15, 1911. Standard was given six months to dissolve. At this time, John D. Archbold was still in charge. He remained active in the oil business until he died on December 5, 1916, of complications following an operation for appendicitis at age sixty-eight.

Several qualities are apparent as one reads about his life. He had a great sense of humor, which many said was important in his rise to power in the oil business and especially the affairs of Standard Oil. He apparently never felt frustrated, nor did he give up his independence. It was later revealed that he also had several favorite charities, including the American Museum of Natural History where his grandson was to have much success. Another of his favorites was Syracuse University, then a smallish Methodist college where rules against drinking, gambling, card playing, and dancing were strictly enforced in accordance with the sect's philosophy. He served on the Syracuse University Board of Trustees and was at one time chairman of the board. Under his guidance, and that of his hand-selected university president, the number of colleges grew from three to eight and the endowment to several million. He is reported to have contributed $6 million to the university and was responsible for the building of a men's dormitory, a gymnasium, and Archbold Stadium.

The First and Second New Guinea Expeditions

The First Expedition

The idea of supporting an exploration of New Guinea was born sometime during the period between Archbold's return trip from Madagascar and his first few months in New York. On his way home, he met Sanford (of the American Museum) in Europe, and they discussed what kind of biological exploration needed to be done in the world. Archbold records on page 44 of his autobiographical notes that "I wanted to go on with it," meaning exploration. His office in the American Museum was across the hall from that of Ernst Mayr,[4] an ornithologist who had arrived recently from Germany and who had made one trip to New Guinea. Leonard Sanford introduced Archbold to Mayr and suggested that they could probably help each other. Mayr was aware of the diversity of the fauna and flora in New Guinea and inspired Archbold to undertake an expedition there. The pair made a trip to the Archbold family home in Georgia and talked about what was to be done. Mayr records their trip and his relationship with Archbold in the following vignette, taken from his typed notes in the station archives.

When I arrived at the American Museum in January 1931, the desk among the collection cases where I worked was in the North Wing on the fifth floor. On the other side, across the hall, was the mammal department. One of the workers there was Richard Archbold, a grandson of one of John D. Rockefeller's associates. Soon after my arrival, Dr. Leonard Sanford introduced Dick Archbold to me, presumably with two ideas in mind (Sanford was forever scheming!). First of all, Dick was a bit awkward and had few, if any, friends. Sanford thought it would be nice for him to know me and equally for me, who at that time didn't know anyone in New York, to know young Archbold. We didn't become very intimate, but we saw each other frequently. One day in the fall of 1931, Dick asked me, "Have you ever been to the South?" I admitted that I hadn't. "Wouldn't you be interested to visit it?" he then asked. "Yes," I said, "but I am afraid I wouldn't be able to afford it." "Well," he said, "it gives me great pleasure to invite you to be my companion when I fly to Thomasville, Georgia, later this fall." I happily accepted this invitation, being quite touched by his kindness and generosity.

We left New York early in the morning and first flew to Washington, D.C. There we took a smaller plane that seated only about eight people and made one or two stops in every state between D.C. and Florida. As a result, we reached our destination, Jacksonville, only after dark.

From South Carolina on, Dick and I were the only passengers, and Dick asked the pilot to fly over the estuaries and marshes near the coastline. As a result, we had a marvelous view of the wintering ducks and geese. In Jacksonville we were met by a limousine, and the chauffeur drove us to Thomasville. Dick's father's plantation was quite a wonderful place. The wildlife specialist who was in charge of propagating quail (and maybe also turkeys), Herb Stoddard, showed us around the place and told us everything about raising quail. On a later day he drove us to Tallahassee, which, at that time, was a lovely, quiet, country town full of huge, stately live and water oaks with lots of Spanish moss hanging down. He also took us to Wakulla Springs, at that time not yet discovered by tourists. I had my first very close view of limpkins and other rare waterbirds. Finally, he took us to the Gulf coast to a place called Shell Point, where we saw lots of shore and seabirds.

In Thomasville, Dick was considered a VIP citizen, and he belonged to all the local clubs, et cetera. He took me to one of the meetings of a Lions or Rotary Club (I forgot which). I was introduced and asked to report about Germany. As far as a southern state was concerned, this was very soon after the war and I felt, in spite of all apparent politeness, a considerable remnant of hostility. On this trip Dick was always concerned that I should really enjoy myself. This he did himself, quite evidently, owing to his love for nature.

After our return to New York, I regularly dropped in on Dick in his apartment on Central Park West, I believe in the same building as the Explorer's Club. I usually went there at cocktail hour to have a drink with Dick.

In 1932, Dick invited me to come with him for some mountaineering in Switzerland. His plans for that year included the Matterhorn. Unfortunately, I had to decline, being notoriously acrophobic, regretting intensely not to be able to go with Dick. With his courage and determination, apparently, no mountain was too difficult for Dick.

Austin Rand, Dick's companion on so many expeditions, was not around the American Museum at that time. I believe he was in Ithaca working for his Ph.D. at Cornell.

From 1932 on, when I had been appointed curator of the Witney Rothschild Collections, I was exceptionally busy and my companionship with Dick suffered. However, I had inspired him to explore New Guinea, and this became the center of his interest in the ensuing years.

Soon after Dick had established the Lake Placid station in Florida, he invited me to visit him there some late spring. No scientific work was as yet going on there, but Dick was in love with the country. He took me on long drives to Lake Okeechobee, to some large cypress swamps, and we had a wonderful time watching birds and other wildlife. At that time, Florida was much wilder than it is now.

After 1953, when I had accepted the Agassiz professorship at Harvard, I saw Dick much more rarely. However, I had friends in Tampa, Punta Gorda, and Port Everglades, and whenever I visited these friends I always made it a point to visit the Archbold Station and, if possible, to stay for a few days. Dick was a gracious host, and there was always something interesting to see.

The news of his death in 1976 greatly saddened me. Dick was only three years younger than I, and we had thought of ourselves as contemporaries. I shall always have a warm memory of Dick. In his deep interests, generosity, public spiritedness, and modesty, he was a truly admirable person.

Finding a Botanist

Archbold notes that one of the deficiencies in the Madagascar expedition was that he and his colleagues did not know what the animals they collected ate and it was therefore appropriate to bring a botanist on the trip to New Guinea. Interestingly, he records that he might have taken an entomologist but that he felt that botany was the more basic science (though he wrote that little was known about both New Guinea botany and entomology).

To find a botanist, he consulted with a Dr. Barrel, who was director of the Bronx Botanical Garden and a Dr. White, a librarian in Brisbane, Australia. They recommended Leonard J. Brass of Australia (see appendix); he joined the team in Port Moresby at the outset of the first New Guinea expedition. Archbold and Rand (1939) later wrote that Brass, "besides being a competent botanist and pleasant associate, was experienced in the ways of camp life and knew native customs." Brass remained with Archbold through the three New Guinea expeditions, moved with him to Florida, and led a postwar expedition to the Cape York area of Australia and two more to New Guinea. (Cape York is the closest piece of Australian land next to New Guinea.) Brass retired from the Archbold station and American Museum staffs in 1966 and returned to Australia.

Why Fly? Learning to Fly

The first New Guinea expedition was a grand success, and a great number of plant and animal specimens were obtained for the American Museum of Natural History's collections. Archbold wrote that he wanted to undertake another expedition. However, to reach the interior and the mountains of New Guinea would require several hundred native carriers, with the concomitant problems of logistics, government red tape, possible sickness among the carriers, and especially difficulties with warring factions (both among the carriers and between the carriers and those who lived on the land where the party might pass). Rand and Brass (1940) wrote, "What makes New Guinea an extremely difficult country to penetrate is that local natives cannot be depended on to act as carriers." This statement should not be interpreted to mean local people were lazy, for that was not the case. Rather, because of the warfare between tribes, local people did not dare to venture into a neighboring tribe's territory. Further, and on the other hand, Archbold and Rand (1939) recorded that "if perchance a native tribe had an abundant harvest, they are apt to have invited all of the neighboring tribes for a feast and dance and to have eaten all of the surplus, leaving nothing for the traveler."

Archbold and Rand agreed that the best way to reach the interior of New Guinea was by airplane. However, Archbold wrote later, "When I originally went into aviation I had no idea of going into it in quite as large a scale as it wound up to be." It is clear that at this point an airplane was merely a matter of convenience to aid the expeditions; nobody wanted to establish any world flight records.

Soon after their return from the first New Guinea expedition, Archbold learned to fly in a Curtis Bentley airplane owned by O. J. Whitney and housed at North Beach, Long Island. Flying with others, being a student pilot, and watching the mechanics overhaul engines soon became an everyday affair. "I succeeded in picking up a small amphibian, Keystone Commuter"—"it was a slow thing." From there he graduated to a number of other planes. It was during this time that he met Russell Rogers, who became his pilot and companion in flight for several years.

The *Kono*

The plane selected for the second expedition was a Fairchild Amphibian Model 91 that had one Wright Cyclone engine and a wingspan of sixty-seven feet. It could carry a payload of 4,000 pounds and had sufficient fuel to fly 1,300 miles. It was a true amphibian. With an airspeed of 140 miles per hour, it could land on lakes and rivers as well as dry ground, though there were only a few airports on the island of New Guinea. Archbold called the plane the *Kono*.[5]

With such a short flight range, it was necessary to ship the plane, much of it neatly crated, by freighter to Brisbane, Australia; there it was assembled and flown to Daru, where the coastal base for the expedition was established. Several reconnaissance flights were made over the area to be explored. Archbold wrote they were often flying over countryside "which we had trudged and sweated for so many weary hours two years before." After a period of exploration, camps were established on the upper parts of the Fly River.

The research and collections were making good progress when the *Kono* sank while at anchor in Port Moresby in a severe predawn storm, locally called a "guba." This was four and a half months after the starting date of the insurance policy under which the plane was covered. An effort was made to save the *Kono,* but this only resulted in further damage. Part of the plane protruded above the water and was a threat to local navigation. In order to avoid paying unreasonably high importation taxes, Archbold had it towed into deeper waters and a deep-sea grave in international waters. Several parts, including the propeller, were salvaged before the plane was sunk.

However, the affair was not a total loss for one of the several insurance companies involved, which paid the claim. The Publicity Department of the Royal Insurance Company Limited of New York asked Archbold for a picture of the plane with the New Guinea natives sitting on the wings. They proposed to use it in an ad in an insurance in-house trade publication. The proposed ad's first line, submitted to Archbold for approval, read, "New Guinea (just north of Australia and part of the one-time Cannibal Islands Group) is one of the wild frontiers of the world." I have not been able to find any proof that the ad was published.

The Second Expedition

The exploits of the second expedition to New Guinea are condensed in two easy-to-read reports by Archbold and Rand (1939) and Rand and Brass (1940). The area where the party was to work was the forested country of the headwaters of the more than 650-mile-long Fly River. This is the largest river in New Guinea and drains country that had been little visited by outsiders. The mountains at the headwaters are about 10,000 feet tall. Archbold and Rand (1939) wrote, "We hoped to collect at 2,000-foot intervals from 3,000 feet to 10,000 feet."

Archbold and Rand (1939) reported that the people along the mouth of the Fly River had contact with the outside world for a number of years, but the middle Fly people were "formerly notorious raiders, coming far down the river to raid villages in their head hunting expeditions." The people living on the upper reaches of the Fly River lived in the Stone Age; they appeared friendly. Still, Archbold and Rand wrote, "Their women and children never appeared and until the women and children of a bush people appear in camp you have not fully gained their confidence."

Two camps, supplied largely by air, were established successfully on the upper reaches of the Fly River, and considerable collecting was done from both. The party was in the process of establishing a third camp at the base of Mt. Blucher when disaster struck and the plane sank on July 8, 1936. Archbold was on the coast with the plane when it sank, but he was in radio contact with Rand and the rest of the party. Rand wrote, "The immediate problem confronting us was a safe and speedy retreat to a place on the river where we could receive supplies by boat." Only a small amount of collecting was done from the camp at the base of the mountains, so "we had a small representation of the mountain fauna."

To move down the river, the explorers built several rafts. Four, two-foot diameter, twenty-foot-long logs were cut and lashed together to make a single raft. Selection of the trees to be cut had to done with care since not all of the trees in the forests had trunks that would float. The ten or eleven rafts held five scientists, sixty natives, and two dogs. Rand reported, "Tate had his rats on his raft, Brass his plants on his, and I had my birds on mine." Some of the rafts carried more than 1,500 pounds, including one American and five or six native porters and their camp gear. The members of the party had seen the river from the air and were aware they had to pass through some rapids and whirlpools. There was also some flooding during their journey downstream, and at one point the "turbulent river had a nine-knot current." Rand wrote that his raft went crashing through some lodged timber and afterward it was "more diamond shaped than square," but fortunately it stayed together, was easily repaired, and no bird specimens were lost. One of the porters' rafts was caught in a whirlpool, but "a sudden up-swelling of water spewed it out into the current again."

After nearly a month of rafting (and collecting), the crew reached Oroville, a gold prospector's camp. During their journey downriver they had frequent radio contact with Archbold, who was coming up-river on a relief ship, the *Ronald S.* They waited in Oroville for the boat, which arrived on August 10. Archbold brought with him sufficient supplies for three months. The team decided to work the lowlands of South New Guinea "intensively" from the shores of the Fly River. After a few more days Archbold and the radio operator left for home, leaving Rand, Brass, and Tate, together with some local police to protect them. The collecting went well, and several observations of bird behavior were made, so the expedition was profitable despite the change in plans. Archbold and Rand (1939) noted that the area was changing rapidly even in the short time they were there. Gold and oil prospectors were moving into Daru and up the Fly River in numbers. Rand and most of the remainder of the party left for home on February 16, 1937, arriving in New York in March. Meanwhile, Richard Archbold was back home making plans and laying the groundwork for an even more ambitious third expedition to New Guinea. Most of those involved in the second expedition to New Guinea were in the field from February 1936 through March 1937.

Incorporation of Biological Explorations

All of the Archbold expeditions had been financed through and under the auspices of the American Museum of Natural History. Moneys for the expedition to Madagascar and for the first and second expeditions to New Guinea had been direct gifts to the museum from the Archbolds. Upon Richard Archbold's return to the United States in 1936, a nonprofit corporation, Biological Explorations, was established to fund future expeditions.

Biological Explorations was organized under the laws of the Commonwealth of Pennsylvania. (Both Archbold Expeditions and the Archbold Biological Station still operate today within this corporation since grandfathered into the original agreement were broad guidelines that continue to be useful.) The articles of incorporation state that the purpose is to "finance, organize, undertake and conduct a scientific expedition or expeditions for the purpose of exploring scientifically and making biological, ethnological, geological and geographical investigations of remote, undisclosed and comparatively little-known regions." Such expeditions may be conducted in the United States as well as in other countries. The directors have the authority "to make, alter, amend and repeal the bylaws." The term of the corporation is "perpetual." The charter was approved by the court on March 12, 1937.

Five of the original directors of the corporation were apparently attorneys acting in Archbold's interests, but Adrian Archbold, Richard's younger brother, was a director and treasurer. This changed on July 21, 1937, after Rand returned from New Guinea, when the elected directors became Richard Archbold (president), Archbold Van Beuren (vice president), Adrian Archbold (secretary and treasurer), Austin L. Rand, and Harold E. Anthony.

The office of Biological Explorations was in Philadelphia, but it was also stated in the articles of incorporation that there could be an office at 26 Broadway in New York City, the longtime address of the Standard Oil Corporation. On July 20, 1937, under the address 26 Broadway, Richard Archbold turned over to Biological Explorations a number of shares of stock, an airplane, Consolidated-boat NC 777, cameras, and miscellaneous equipment in exchange for 500 shares of stock in Biological Explorations, that being "all the authorized capitol stock of the corporation." The address of the corporation continued to be 26 Broadway through 1938; in 1939 the office was moved to 30 Rockefeller Plaza, which was also the location of the Archbold family office.

The Third New Guinea Expedition

Guba I and *II*

The *Kono,* the amphibious aircraft, had proven its worth in the second expedition to New Guinea, but something larger and more air-worthy was needed for the third expedition, which was to explore at higher altitudes. As they were returning by ship from the second expedition, Archbold and Rogers checked aviation magazines for new aircraft that would be useful to them; they rejected several models. Archbold (1939) reported that upon returning home he was contacted by the Consolidated Aircraft Corporation of San Diego, which had heard he was in the market for a flying boat. At the time, Consolidated had a large order for amphibian aircraft from the navy, and the model it wanted to sell him was the first of its kind. This model was on the restricted list, which meant it could not be resold or taken out of the country without navy approval. Such restrictions did not deter Archbold, who proceeded to have one rebuilt to his specifications.

Archbold took delivery of *Guba I* at Boulder Dam (now the Hoover Dam on the Colorado River on the Arizona-Nevada border) so as to avoid paying California sales tax. He proceeded to take test flights, including flying in and out of Lake Tahoe to check its performance at higher altitudes. The plane was brought east over the mild objections of the War Department. Several shakedown cruises of *Guba I* followed, including one to Cuba. One reason for the several shakedown cruises was that Archbold and Rogers were testing candidates for the job of navigator; after rejecting several, they settled on Lewis A. Yancey, who proved to be an excellent choice.

Fate now intervened. The Russians needed a heavy-duty plane to search for one of theirs that was lost trying to fly from Moscow over the North Pole to the United States. Archbold's flying boat was thought to be the only machine capable of undertaking a search in such a cold country. A special meeting of the directors of Biological Explorations was held on August 17, 1937, to approve the sale of the *Guba I* back to Consolidated with the understanding that Biological Explorations would receive from Consolidated a new plane, which was to be an improved version "equipped in every respect similar to the airplane being exchanged, by November 1, 1937." The new plane proved to have several advantages as a result of the first shakedown cruises. (The Soviets searched but never found their downed crew.) It is interesting that the navy, which was reluctant for Archbold to purchase the plane in the beginning, did nothing to stop the sale to the Soviets.

Guba II, with pilots Richard Archbold and Russell Rogers, navigator Yancey, radioman Raymond E. Booth, and flight engineers Stephen Barinka and Gerald D. Brown, left San Diego for New Guinea on a much publicized takeoff on June 2, 1938. The route took the plane and its crew to Hawaii, Wake Island, and Hollandia (Kotabaru) in northern Dutch New Guinea. They arrived on June 10. The purpose, as we all know, was the exploration of the interior of New Guinea. However, world politics, the newness of international air travel, and the coming

Guba, a navy-designed bomber redesigned by Richard Archbold for exploration purposes. Note the Archbold insignia on the plane. Station archives.

new war all impinged on what was intended to be a purely scientific venture.

Guba II, like *Guba I*, was a twin-engine flying boat built as a long-range bombing machine. The plane weighed thirteen tons, and Archbold's copy was the largest privately owned aircraft in the world. It was powered by twin 900-horsepower engines but could fly on one. It had a maximum speed of 190 miles per hour and a range of 4,200 miles. Though much of the trip around the world was over uncharted waters, the ship had excellent radios and was in constant touch with the outside world. This model, called a PBY, proved to be a durable aircraft, and some forty planes of the original design are still flying today.

Guba II returned to New York, and a hero's welcome at the New York World's Fair, on July 1, 1939, having taken the longest possible path, close to the equator and across Africa, around the earth. In a cooperative agreement with the Australians, it left Port Headland in northwestern Australia and stopped at Batavia (Jakarta), the capital of the Dutch East Indies (having been diverted there because the Cocos Islands were fogged in), the Cocos Islands, Diego Garcia, and the Seychelles, all

Guba's crew, left to right: flight engineer Stephen Barrinka, navigator Lewis A. Yancey, Richard Archbold, pilot Russell R. Rogers, radioman Raymond E. Booth, and flight engineer Gerald D. Brown just before their takeoff for New Guinea on June 2, 1938. Station archives.

islands in the Indian Ocean under British command, and on to Mombassa on the coast of Kenya, the Belgian Congo, Dakar in the French West Indies, St. Thomas in the Virgin Islands, and home to New York. Three countries elected to commemorate *Guba*'s exploits with several postage stamps (see appendix for details).

Lowell Thomas, at the time (1940) a well-known radio commentator and writer, had glowing words about Archbold's around-the-world flight. He wrote: "There was an ocean"—the Indian Ocean—"that no one had ever flown before—he flew it. There was a vast jungle that no white man had ever entered—he explored it. Yet few people have even heard of Richard Archbold—publicity scares him." Thomas continued: "If you press him to give an account of his experiences he will tell them with all the color and vividness of a man reading from a telephone directory. But men like to be with him in a tough spot because they find him not only an imperturbable leader but a master of unforeseen situations."

The Expedition

The third expedition was to that part of New Guinea controlled by the Netherlands. It was the most ambitious and successful of the Archbold expeditions and was a joint venture between the Dutch and the Americans with the official name Indisch-Amerikaansche Expeditie. The Dutch provided military personnel, an entomologist, Dr. L. J. Toxopeus, and a forester, Dr. E. Meyer-Drees, both of whom were accompanied by assistants, including two Sudanese mantris (trained native insect collectors). The military included a captain, three lieutenants (one of whom was a physician), fifty-two noncommissioned officers and men, and thirty convict carriers. The military were thought necessary because so few Europeans had visited the area and it was little known. The American Museum group included Archbold, Rand, Brass, mammalogist W. B. Richardson, three collectors, forty-two carriers, and two cooks in addition to the pilot, navigator, radioman, and two mechanics. The total party, including some hired locally, was nearly

Richard Archbold in the pilot's seat in *Guba*. Station archives.

200 people. The expedition was in the field from April 1938 to May 1939.

A detailed report of the expedition was prepared by Archbold, Rand, and Brass (1948), though a more romantic and readable account was prepared by Archbold (1941). There is also an unpublished 116-page manuscript in the American Museum of Natural History and Archbold Biological Station files by Archbold and Tate that gives an even more detailed report about the Grand Valley, a remote area with a more advanced culture. A number of articles were published as a result of specimens collected on this expedition. Of special interest is Rand's 1940 account of the courtship of a bird of paradise, which he watched from a palm leaf shelter only an arm's length away.

The work area was the north slope of the Snow Mountains, which had been the least studied part of the entire island. The expedition worked out of several camps but was always in radio contact with the base camp in Hollandia. One of the first steps after Archbold arrived on the site was to erect buildings to house people and supplies. This was done using raised concrete floors from previous buildings that had been built when Hollandia flourished as a center for bird of paradise hunters. Provisioning of the inland parties was accomplished either by the plane's landing on lakes and rivers or via parachute. In this expedition, the team first explored and collected from the highest, most inland areas and from there worked back to the coast.

In addition to the collecting of plants and animals in this part of New Guinea, several other aspects of the explorations proved fruitful. One was the landing of *Guba II* on Lake Habbema at an altitude of 3,225 meters (11,342 feet) and about 180 miles from the main base at Hollandia. The highest elevation tested by *Guba II* prior to this time was Lake Tahoe's elevation of about 7,500 feet. The landing at Lake Habbema was of special interest to the navy, for whom the plane had been designed. No one had ever landed and taken off with an amphibian plane at such a height, and the aircraft itself had never been tested under

Guba on Lake Habbema in New Guinea. Mt. Wilhelmina is in the background. Station archives.

such high conditions. "On July 15, 1938, with Archbold, Rogers, Booth, Brown and Yancey as crew, food supplies for two months, tents, arms, a radio set, a collapsible boat, a buoy and some spare gasoline, a trial landing was made on Lake Habbema" (Archbold, Rand, and Brass 1948). The lake looked shallow, and to check the depth of the water, the party attached several sinkers to five feet of rope and dropped a buoy where the plane proposed to land. All of the buoys disappeared, and the party thought it safe to land, which they did with ease. "Experimental takeoffs" showed the plane could take off easily carrying a payload of 1,000 kilograms (2,200 pounds), while a load of 3,000 kilograms (6,600 pounds) could be landed. Many flights during July brought in the needed 105 people and supplies (450,000 pounds), and the collections were under way.

The camp had one full month's rations and reserves for an additional two months. When their camp was finished and ready for work, the group took a holiday. The date was July 31. They raised the Dutch flag, and Archbold and Dutch Captain Teerink made speeches.

New York City mayor Fiorello La Guardia (center) and Richard Archbold (right) examine a map to trace the round-the-world trip by *Guba II* in July 1939. The naval officer on the left is unknown. Station archives.

In the next month, a camp was established at an even higher altitude of 3,560 meters (10,000 feet). At the same time the military was conducting several patrols. In general, the people were friendly and offered food, especially pigs, which were apparently a staple in their diets. In some cases the natives were armed with bows and spears, and while at first aloof, they soon became friendly when offered seashells. Archbold (1941) reported that some of the native groups with whom they visited had "many scars from arrow wounds on their bodies," which suggested they were more warfaring, though this was not true of all the local tribes. In some instances, according to Archbold, "we found evidence among them of ceremonial cannibalism." In one case, a large knife was stolen from a patrol, but it was later returned and friendly relations were resumed. Still, it was obvious that keeping a large force together was the safest and most practical way to avoid trouble.

During the following month a concentrated effort was made to collect at elevations above Lake Habbema. There were also several attempts, led by Archbold, to climb to the peak of Mt. Wilhelmina, all of which failed because of poor weather. The highest collecting camp was established at this time at 3,800 meters. The work was made easier by using native trails that could be found throughout the areas. The collecting continued but was often made impossible because of the weather, especially the cold, wet days. The camps at the higher elevations were slowly abandoned, and efforts again concentrated around Lake Habbema. The explorations continued, but during the next few months the camps were moved to lower elevations and closer to the coast. The expedition finished its work in April and May of 1939 with the *Guba II* departing on May 12 and the very last of the party leaving Hollandia by steamer on May 21.

The Grand Valley

Upon their arrival in New Guinea the Archbold party began to make reconnaissance flights over the territory to be explored. In the process they came upon the unknown Grand Valley. This valley is approximately 3,000 feet high, 80 kilometers long, and 20 kilometers wide; running through it is the Balim River. It is home to an estimated 60,000 people living unlike any others in New Guinea. This proved to be one of the interesting sociological discoveries of the third expedition. Unlike natives in the rest of New Guinea, the Grand Valley people had large fields and gardens walled with stone, and from the air the sight reminded Archbold of parts of Europe. Archbold et al. (1948) wrote that the fields were of "pleasing native irregularity." The Grand Valley had been deforested and used for farming up to elevations of 2,300 or 2,400 feet above the valley floor because so many people lived there. Most of the other gardens that Archbold had seen in New Guinea were weedy patches in small clearings.

Some of the valley was low-lying and swampy, and here the natives had built broad drainage ditches. The villages were walled or stockaded. Still, these were Stone Age people who did not know about the wheel and used only crude stone implements and a few steel knives that had found their way to the interior via trading. There were no beasts of burden. Their chief garden plants were sweet potatoes, taro, sugarcane, and bananas. Smallish pigs appeared to be the chief source of meat.

Archbold found that when he and members of his party met the people of the Grand Valley that they were usually unarmed and friendly. They had cut down the forest with stone axes and scorned gifts of steel ones. They used heavy wooden poles wielded by hand for plows and cultivators. Archbold was also impressed with the fact that they appeared to understand the dangers of erosion on the side hills and cultivated these accordingly. The natives had built several impressive suspension bridges across the Balim River that were made of tree branches and limbs held together with rattan.

The Military Air Crash

In May 1945, near the end of World War II, the Grand Valley was the site of a U.S. Air Force transport plane crash in which twenty of the twenty-three people on board were killed. Reports on rescuing the remaining three people were prime-time radio news for several weeks. The Grand Valley was dubbed Shangri-la by the survivors, who thought they were the first outsiders to visit the area. Like Archbold, the surviving soldiers were impressed with the friendliness of the natives.

In a broadcast on September 19, 1945, Martin Agronsky, at the time a well-known radio commentator, reported that Archbold had been there first and that the rescue operations "were needlessly thrilling, that they were needlessly prolonged, that the rescue could have been performed a lot more quickly and a lot more safely." Agronsky said that the army had in its file-and-forget file, plans for a rescue operation that were included in Richard Archbold's report on his expedition to the War Department. Archbold was much more conscious of the importance of contingency plans after the loss of the *Kono* in the second expedition and had several ready for use, if necessary, by those people on the third.

The Sale and Fate of *Guba*

The final fate of *Guba* was neatly summarized by Adkisson (1996–97), the source of the account in this section. Germany invaded Poland only two months after the expedition returned home, and it was evident there would not be another expedition in the near future. The plane was sold to the British and flown by a Royal Air Force crew to Scotland. It was flown at an altitude of 15,000 feet (5,000 meters), and icing created a hazardous situation. Pieces of ice from the props were slung off, breaking the window by the navigator's station. The plane was unheated. and apparently the crew suffered greatly from the cold. At one point *Guba* broke cloud cover and watched as the British liner, the *Empress of Britain,* sank after being attacked by a German plane, which fortunately did not know *Guba* was nearby.

Guba was assigned to spotting and bombing German submarines. Later, it was assigned to the Transport Command moving military personnel first to Gibraltar and later to ports along the West African coast. The plane managed to avoid the Luftwaffe but was caught in a severe storm somewhere along the African coast in 1944 and was damaged beyond repair. The British cabled Archbold and reported it was being towed out to sea and sunk.

Disease and Health Problems

Articles reporting the successes of the Archbold expeditions to Madagascar and New Guinea fail to mention one fact: the explorers suffered from repeated bouts with disease, especially malaria. Disease was never mentioned in any of the expedition members' reports; nor did they complain about this in any of the articles they wrote. The popular reports of the expeditions, especially in *Natural History* magazine, were romantic portrayals and did not mention any adverse side effects. In fact, however, disease was a serious problem for the explorers. I learned this information while having a conversation with Frances Hufty, Richard Archbold's sister, who said, "They all went to the hospital upon returning home to recover."

However, the truth comes to light in Archbold's June, 1, 1960–April 15, 1961, annual station report to the American Museum, in which it is stated in a routine, factual style that Brass suffered from "chronic vivax malaria" from mid-March to mid-December. The report for the next year, dated April 27, 1962, states that Brass "was again severely handicapped by illness"—"by a recurrence of malaria contracted in New Guinea in 1959." The problem continued, and the report dated April 19, 1963, reports that Brass "had indifferent health, which again limited his work." We can assume that this too was a result of malaria. We know today that it takes three years to make a full recovery from malaria. In the earlier, June 22, 1955, annual report, it is noted that Dr. Geoffrey M. Tate, who worked out of the American Museum in New York City, retired that year as a result of a "totally and permanently" debilitating stroke suffered while on the 1953 expedition to New Guinea. With prompt medical attention, Tate might have fared better in his recovery. Exploration definitely has its downside!

The Archbold Biological Station:
The Early Years

The Arizona Expedition

As international tensions grew in 1939 and 1940, it became apparent that a fourth expedition to New Guinea would need to be postponed. As a result, an effort was made to establish a field station and residence for Archbold and his group somewhere in the United States. Rand (1941) wrote that "Richard decided to set up a temporary biological station in the United States to keep the Archbold Expedition organization together." Southern Arizona, near Tucson, appealed to Archbold because of his knowledge of the area and his favorable experience while at the Evans School. According to Rand (1941), a temporary headquarters was set up at the Tanque Verde Ranch and "we had a very successful season, studying and photographing wild life in the desert."

I could not find a formal report of the January to June 1940 Arizona expedition, but Rand (1941) wrote about their activities in a popular article in *Natural History* magazine: "We were left with an organization for exploration and no place to explore"—thus it seemed time "to discover facts, not things." Rand's article reviewed the behavioral and photographic studies of desert wildlife that he and Archbold had conducted. One result was the construction of a display of native Arizona life in the hall of North American Mammals of the American Museum of Natural History based on the material they had collected.

Changing Biological Explorations to Archbold Expeditions

At a meeting of the board of directors of Biological Explorations on July 11, 1940, it was agreed to change the name of the organization to Archbold Expeditions. This was approved by the court on August 13, 1940. The name Biological Explorations was in use by another organization. At the same July 11 meeting, the board voted to sell *Guba* and Austin Rand resigned, citing the fact that, because he was a Canadian citizen and Canada, as part of the commonwealth, was at war with Germany, he needed to return to his native country as a loyal citizen.

Acquiring the Roebling Property

Following the Arizona expedition, Archbold had a chance meeting in New York City with an old friend from his school days, Donald Roebling. (The details of this meeting were recorded by Frank A. Rinald, Archbold's longtime secretary [Rinald 1948].) Archbold was told about the Roebling Red Hill estate in Florida developed by Margaret Shippen Roebling, Donald's mother. She had been a student of botany, and now that she was deceased, no one else in the family was interested in the property. The family wanted the property to go to someone who would be "sensitive to the unspoiled beauty of the land." Archbold visited the property and "was impressed with the possibilities of the establishment and its surroundings." The result was that John A. Roebling, Donald's

The "warehouse," which is now the laboratory building, under construction in 1930. Station archives.

father, arranged to sell the property to Archbold for one dollar. Rinald recorded that Helen Price Roebling, John's second wife, had an interest in the land, but I could not confirm this.

The Roebling Family and Their Florida Interests

The idea to acquire the property in Florida and to build a winter home on Red Hill was that of Margaret Shippen Roebling (Mrs. John A. Roebling). John Roebling was the son of Washington A. Roebling and grandson of John Augustus Roebling of Brooklyn Bridge fame and owners of the Roebling Wire and Fence Company of Trenton, New Jersey. Margaret Roebling had tuberculosis and had been advised, for health reasons, to spend her winters in a warm climate. She died suddenly in New Jersey on October 24, 1930. Despite his wife's death, John Roebling continued to develop the Red Hill property that he had purchased for their Florida estate. It was fenced, and the main building that now houses several research laboratories was constructed. The large

Construction of what is now the laboratory building involved much hand labor. Station archives.

The warehouse in 1935. Station archives.

building would house the equipment and materials needed to build the family residence.

The engineer in charge of the construction on Red Hill and the Highlands Hammock State Park (see below) was Alexander Blair.[6] No effort was made to start construction of the main house that was to have been on the north side of a small, paved circle at the highest point on the hill. To my knowledge, no architect was ever hired, and no one has ever seen any plans. In 1936, Roebling decided to sell, or give away, the Red Hill property. It was refused by a number of people and organizations until it was given to Archbold in 1941. In the interim, Blair continued to oversee the property.

The Highlands Hammock State Park

Margaret Roebling also became interested in what is now the nearly 5,000-acre Highlands Hammock State Park, one of 141 state parks currently owned and operated by the state of Florida. The place was originally known as Hooker Hammock and was named after a Captain Hooker who established a cow camp there. Hooker was a veteran of the Indian wars of the 1840s and 1850s and had been stationed at Fort Meade.

Negotiations to preserve the Highlands Hammock started in 1928 when the National Park Service was contacted by some Sebring residents who recognized the uniqueness of the land. The Park Service responded that the place was too small to be acquired as part of its system. Donald Roebling, who was pilot, flew his mother over the hammock in February 1930. She was impressed with the natural beauty of the area and inquired about plans for its acquisition. She subsequently offered the first money for the purchase of what was then a 500-acre tract. Equally important, she had Alexander Blair, the engineer in charge of construction on the Red Hill property, represent the family concerning the negotiations and plans to develop the park.

Alexander Blair, civil and structural engineer employed by John Roebling to oversee construction of the Red Hill property. Station archives

Fire control became paramount in preserving many of the older trees and other plants in the park after a disastrous fire on Easter weekend in 1956. The staff were given fire training, fire lanes were constructed, and Archbold, a member of the advisory council, gave the park its first fire truck. (He was present and worked as a firefighter with his own truck in the 1956 conflagration.)

John Roebling continued his wife's interest in the Highlands Hammock State Park property and funded its development until it was donated to the state. Later, Altvater (1979) wrote a history of the park, and Wilson (unpublished) prepared a more fully researched and documented article on the Red Hill area, especially Hicoria, and the Highlands Hammock State Park.

The Alligator

During World War II, Donald Roebling invented a famous all-steel amphibious vehicle, dubbed "the Alligator," for use as a lifesaving-rescue machine. Trial runs were made on Lake Annie. Roebling's design was used to make amphibious troop carriers used by the marines for island hopping in the Pacific during World War II.

A paragraph in a letter from Alexander Blair to John A. Roebling dated April 28, 1942, and found with the papers associated with the Red Hill abstract, reads, "The annual Meeting of the [Florida Engineering] Society was held in Tampa last week. Thanks to the kindly offices of Donald [Roebling] and of Colonel Davies of the U.S. Marines, a number of the engineers of Florida were permitted to make a trip in one of the new steel amphibians at the proving grounds in Dunedin. This was an experience which these men all thoroughly enjoyed and appreciated."

Roebling's alligator. Photo by A. Blair.

Richard Archbold (left), Marie Brass, Dr. Leonard Brass, and Donald Roebling at the station in 1945. Station archives.

The Deed to Red Hill

On May 15, 1929, John A. Roebling purchased from the Consolidated Land Company all of sections 7 and 8 lying east of the Atlantic Coast Line Railroad Company right-of-way in township 38 of Highlands County with the exception of the road right-of-way between Lake Annie[7] and Hicoria.[8] On March 30, 1930, he purchased, again from Consolidated, the southern halves of sections 5 and 6 in the same township with the same exception. (A section is a unit of land that is one-thirty-sixth of a township, or one square mile, or 640 acres.) On July 21, 1941, John A. Roebling and his second wife deeded the above property to Archbold Expeditions as an "absolute, unqualified and unrestricted gift."

No mention is made in the deed of the total acreage. A Highlands County tax bill for 1941, and paid by Roebling, spells out the acreage as follows:

Section 5	314.91 acres
Section 6	4.47 acres
Section 7	99 acres
Section 8	640 acres (a full section)
Total	1,058.38 acres

The acreage stated in other documents and letters varies from 1,000 to 1,065. The tax bill is probably as accurate as any other document.

For those interested in history, the nearly half-inch-thick property abstract that reviews how Consolidated came to own the property begins, "Under the treaty of 1821 with Spain, by which the United States acquired 'The Floridas'," and continues, "The Act of Congress approved March 3, 1845, admitting Florida into the Union of States," et cetera.

In a letter to Archbold dated April 10, 1941, Alexander Blair wrote that "following our conversation of yesterday, on behalf of Mr. John A. Roebling, of Bernardsville, New Jersey, I am authorized to offer to Archbold Expeditions as an absolute, unconditional and unrestricted gift from Mr. Roebling, his property known as 'Red Hill.'. . . Mr. Roebling is willing to extend to you the privilege of using the property until the execution of the deed." Blair worked with Archbold's Miami attorneys to satisfy Archbold's two concerns: first, that the property be considered a gift as "provided by the Internal Revenue Code," and second, that the property be exempt from real estate taxes. Blair continued as a Roebling employee, and there is no indication that he was ever employed by Archbold.

In a letter dated September 9, 1941, to Alexander Blair, the Atlantic Coast Line Railroad Company canceled the agreement concerning the side track "constructed by and at the expense of John A. Roebling," and the track, which ran the length of the main building on its west side, was removed shortly thereafter. In a letter dated a day earlier, the railroad station name was changed from Red Hill, the name of the station used by the Roeblings, to Archbold.

Prior to giving the property to Archbold, Roebling had made an effort to sell the property or to donate it to a worthy organization. A twenty-six-page "Valuation Report on 'Red Hill' Property Highlands County Florida" prepared by C. Walton Rex, Orlando, Florida, dated August 31,

1938, together with a seven-page "Supplementary Valuation Report" by the same person and dated July 31, 1941, will be found in the station archives. More interesting is a separate, eight-page, undated sales brochure titled "Red Hill—A Unique Florida Property!" prepared by Rex-McGill Investment Company, Orlando, Florida, that presumably accompanied the valuation report. This pamphlet contains a physical description of the property plus twelve pictures that show the pristine nature of the grounds and buildings. The pictures include, among others: the railway siding, the interior of one of the storage rooms, and a west view of the buildings from the water tower. On one page the property is called "A Gentleman's Country Estate." Presumably these three items were prepared to aid in the sale of the property. The brochure states, "The contemplated residence of the owner was not constructed, due to a death in the family."

The Physical Plant in 1941

When the Archbold Biological Station was founded on the Roebling property in 1941, the physical plant was self-contained, with its own power and water plants. Commercial electrical power was not available until 1947. The original 1,050-acre property ranged in elevation from 128 to 222 feet above sea level. The properties surrounding the station were described as "thinly settled." There were approximately one and a half miles of paved road and six miles of clay road on the land. Most of the clay road was around the perimeter of the property. Only remnants of the clay and the road can be seen today.

The fence surrounding the property was made of galvanized wire fabricated in the Roebling mill in New Jersey. The hand-hewn fence posts were made by local residents, who were paid one dollar per post. This was thought to be a bonanza as the people in South Florida suffered greatly during the depression and jobs were few. Some of these posts were later replaced by commercially sawed timber cut from trees on the property. The fence itself was set fifty feet inside the property line with a clay road around the outside. An outer barbed wire fence was constructed later, in the early 1990s, on the property line. The clay road on the south side of the property running east from Old State Road 8, almost to state route 27, was apparently deeded to Highlands County.

The main building was 340 by 40 feet, not including the platforms around three sides of the building. There were living quarters at one end and seven work units, each 40 feet square. The building was designed as a service building for the main house that was to have been built at the highest point of land on Red Hill. Water was pumped from a deep well, passed though a charcoal-lime filter bed and into a 75,000-gallon elevated storage tank. Chlorinating of the water was not done until the 1990s. A mobile firefighting unit that was also available as a free public service to the surrounding residents was housed in a building east of the main building. (There has been no destructive fire on the property since 1930.) The buildings included an eleven-car garage complete with servicing and maintenance equipment. Bedrooms in the main building would accommodate ten people.

Archbold moved immediately to make several changes to accommodate guests and biological experimentation. These included building a dining room on the south end of the main building, a roof over the east ramp, additional garages on the backside (east) of the main garage, a greenhouse, several animal cages, and five one- and two-bedroom cottages. Cottage 6, originally a duplex, was built later. A railing was built on the walkway around the building after Dr. James G. Needham, from Cornell University's entomology department, fell off the platform and broke his arm.

The Advisory Board–Board of Directors

At the July 11, 1940, meeting, Archbold announced that he was thinking about forming an advisory board to supplement the activities of the board of directors. The first informal meeting of the advisory board was held more than a year later, on September 23, 1941, with the first formal meeting following on September 26. Though Rand resigned from the board of directors of Archbold Expeditions because of the war, he remained associated with Archbold Expeditions and the American Museum. (The United States did not enter the conflict until after the attack on Pearl Harbor on December 7, 1941, but Britain and Canada were already at war with Germany.) Rand was later named chairman of the advisory board. At a July 20, 1940, meeting of the board of directors, the future of the corporation was discussed at length, with the consensus being that "unsettled world conditions made it impossible to contemplate an expedition in the future."

Following the formation of the advisory board, meetings of the directors of the corporation occurred less frequently. At a meeting of the board of directors on February 3, 1942, E. D. Merrill and Frank Rinald became directors, Rand having resigned to return to Canada. On April 30, 1957, at a meeting at 30 Rockefeller Plaza, Joseph Mulholland replaced Merrill. At a meeting on November 4, 1957, arrangements were made to give approximately an acre of land on Red Hill to the Florida Board of Forestry for the construction of a fire tower, which was considered to be in the best interest of the station. On October 2, 1964, Richard G. van Gelder was elected to replace Rinald, who had died. At a meeting on October 21, 1974, Frances Archbold Hufty, James N. Layne, Thomas D. Nicholson, and Austin L. Rand were elected to replace Adrian Archbold, Mulholland, and Harold E. Anthony,[9] all of whom had died. Hufty was elected secretary and treasurer.

On May 5, 1978, Frances Archbold Hufty became sole owner of the 500 shares of stock and president of the corporation. The trustees were John Archbold Hufty, Mary Page Hufty, M.D., Page Hufty, Page Lee Hufty, James N. Layne, Ph.D., Carter R. Leidy, Frances Archbold Leidy, Gavin G. K. Letts, Thomas D. Nicholson, Ph.D., and Austin L. Rand, Ph.D.

The Evolution of the Station

How the present station evolved from the Roebling gift is made clear by examining the minutes of one informal and seven formal meetings of the Archbold Biological Station Advisory Board held from September 2, 1941, through October 20, 1944. These minutes were presumably recorded by Frank Rinald. The first two of these meetings preceded the bombing of Pearl Harbor and reflect concerns that existed before the United States entered the war. For the most part, these revolved around the formalities of establishing an outlying station by the American Museum of Natural History, to which Archbold remained firmly attached.

The realities of World War II changed the goals of Archbold Expeditions, as is evident from the minutes of the February 4, 1942, meeting and those that followed. At that meeting Rand resigned from Archbold Expeditions, and Anthony was appointed temporary chairman of the advisory board. Rand was retained as an adviser. Per Host, the only other biologist who had been at the station, was in the military, on leave from Archbold Expeditions. Archbold himself was "engaged in experimental work on instruments to be used by the government in its war effort." He was interested in developing navigational equipment—and had been ever since he had learned to fly a plane. I have been told, but have no documentation to support the claim, that one of the features that attracted him to the Red Hill station was the fact that it had an excellent machine shop (in the northernmost room of the present-day building) where he might work on his inventions.

The minutes for the February 4, 1942, meeting state that "there is no one in charge of biological work and no such work is being done at this time"; that "the Station was established chiefly for the purpose of holding a biological staff together for the duration of the war," with a view to undertaking further New Guinea expeditions when hostilities ceased. It was decided to ask for the cooperation of the museum council about "programs that could be carried on at the Station."

The meeting of the advisory board on September 24, 1942, was "for the purpose of determining what Museum researches might be benefited by work at the Station or in what other ways the facilities of the Station might be advantageously used." However, it was clear that this work was to be done by museum staff and not by people outside that circle.

There were no advisory board meetings in 1943. At the May 31, 1944, meeting it was recorded that "Mr. Archbold's inclinations are about 50/50 in favor of resuming explorations in New Guinea after the war, and maintaining a long-range experimental station in Florida," and he asked the board for advice. The board voted unanimously in favor of "further work in New Guinea" but was also in favor of "constructive and illuminating research" in Florida. What is not mentioned in the minutes, but is clear from other documents, is that Archbold was increasingly becoming involved with the local community including the cooperative electrical company and the preservation of several Florida wildlands.

The October 18, 1944, meeting of the advisory board reflects the stress and uncertainties of the war years. The rationing of gasoline and tires made station life difficult. Archbold expressed concern over his financial ability to support further studies abroad. The possibility of selling the station was discussed. "In response to direct questions, Mr. Archbold said that since the Station plant is already in existence and operating, he inclines to the belief that its development is the more important project." However, he also stated that if business improved and taxes went down after the war, it might be possible to undertake an expedition too. Later, in an addendum to these minutes, he expressed the view that he preferred the alternative of biological work in Florida and he asked the board for advice. It was made clear that the station was well equipped for biological research. The cottages that had been built for the scientific staff and visitors were occupied "by employees who may be expected to live in them while the gas and tire shortage continues."

The minutes of this meeting also note that "in collaboration with Dr. David Fairchild,[10] Mr. Archbold has made experimental plantings of about 300 tropical trees of economic interest, about half of them African mahoganies. . . . There has been a tentative proposal to clear some of the land and plant it to a commercial crop of citrus fruits."

At the seventh board meeting, two days later on October 20, 1944, we see the seeds for the present station being planted. However, Brass referred to a statement he had prepared to the effect that plans for study abroad had "not yet been abandoned."

The *Science* Article and the New Policy

It was at the seventh formal meeting of the advisory board on October 20, 1944, that the present-day station was finally and firmly established. Until this time the use of the station had been restricted to members of the American Museum staff. Brass was directed to prepare an article for *Science* magazine, the official publication of the American Association for the Advancement of Science, which announced to the world the opening of the station to all qualified researchers (Brass 1944). The first paragraph of his article sets forth clear and precise goals:

It is announced by Archbold Expeditions of the American Museum of Natural History that use of the facilities of the Florida station, previously reserved to staff members of the American Museum, will now be extended to a limited number of approved workers from other scientific institutions. The facilities will be available to workers in any field of biological research. A nominal charge to cover living and other expenses is contemplated, but the matter of cost relationships is left open for consideration in accordance with the requirements and circumstances of the studies of each individual.

The remainder of the article reviews the history of Archbold Expeditions and the research conducted at the station to that date. "Inquiries from individuals or institutions" were invited.

A Record of Richard Archbold at the Station

The Post–World War II Years

Rand (1977) wrote that after World War II "Archbold himself took no further active part in the collecting expeditions for mammals and plants after his establishment of the biological station but remained at Red Hill for the rest of his life. He had a small permanent staff and a continual shifting stream of investigators in many aspects of biology [whom he helped by] devising equipment and offering encouragement." One point is clear: while anyone with an interest in biology and natural history was welcome at the station, it was intended primarily as a place of study for senior researchers and their graduate students and for personnel of the American Museum of Natural History.

A record of those who visited the station in the early years was kept on index cards by Archbold's longtime secretary, Frank Rinald, and later appeared in the annual reports made to the American Museum of Natural History. These annual reports began only in early 1957, and the first report covers the period 1941 through 1957 in just three and a quarter, double-spaced pages. Archbold wrote in this report that by 1951 a "pattern of 'returning visitors' was being set" and that "scientists liked working here." He also noted, "High schools in the county were sending their biology classes to the station and we prepared special programs for them."

Archbold continued his strong support of the American Museum of Natural History both during and after World War II. This included covering the costs of an Archbold curator and an office for this person in the mammal department as well as several expeditions to Southeast Asia with an emphasis on New Guinea (see appendix).

According to annual reports from the station proper, in the 1950s, 1960s, and until his death in the 1970s an average of about forty scientists, often with their graduate students, representing thirteen to twenty-two institutions visited the station each year. A number of these people did research there while on sabbatical; others brought their students and conducted one- or two-week-long classes in field biology. He

Richard Archbold talking to a group of Highlands County grade school students in 1970. Photo by J. Layne.

also financed the building of two "habitat" groups of New Guinea and its bird life in the museum's Hall of Oceanic Birds.

The Acquisition of Additional Land

Archbold was repeatedly approached by local people to buy their land. He steadfastly refused such invitations (Wadlow, personal communication). Through the 1950s the human population of Florida did not exceed three million people, and no one could have predicted that it would increase so rapidly in the following decades.

However, the station owns three small satellite pieces of donated land that are available as study sites. In 1952, Dr. Henry T. Price, a Lake Placid pediatrician, and his wife gave Archbold Expeditions an eight-acre parcel on the northern shore of nearby Lake Placid. The tract contains a variety of soil types and associated plant communities including a small black gum swamp near the lake that is one of the better examples of this type of plant life in the area. Other gifts of land not contiguous with station property include an eight-acre tract of deep muck soil on the south end of Lake Istokpoga given by Bert G. Harris III of Lake Placid in 1984. Malcolm and Jeanne Watters of Lake Placid donated a little over sixteen acres, which are predominately low grassy marsh, between Lakes Henry and June-in-Winter in 1988 (Lohrer, unpublished).

A major change in station policy was announced in the 1973–74 annual report when Archbold Expeditions acquired 1,574 acres of undeveloped land west of the railroad bed but contiguous with the station property. These lands are the home of a substantial population of Florida scrub jays that were already under study by Professor Glen E. Woolfenden, research associate at the station and research professor at the University of South Florida. The purchase of this land shows that the station recognized the need for additional property to act as a buffer against encroachment by the expanding human population of Florida; it also served to increase the habitat diversity in the station property.

Dean Amadon's Recollections

In the following remarks, Dean Amadon of the American Museum of Natural History describes his experiences at the Archbold Biological Station and his memories of its founder. (Note that I have altered some capitalization and other minor elements of style in the following excerpt so that it would match the style in the rest of this book.)

> I joined the bird department of the American Museum . . . in 1937. In early 1943, the head of that department, Dr. R. C. Murphy, spoke to me approximately as follows: "A Mr. Richard Archbold has founded a biological research station in Florida. Archbold has sponsored major expeditions through the museum. He and others are anxious to have something published based on work done at the Archbold station. Can you go down there? I am sure you will find a suitable project."
>
> It was wartime, public transportation was difficult; I was 1-A in the draft; my wife and I were celebrating the birth of our first child. However, the draft board gave me permission, and I arrived in Lake Placid after tiring train rides (no berths available). According to the twenty-two-page paper that resulted, "A Preliminary Life History Study of the Florida Jay," I was in Florida from March 27 until April 19. The paper is number 50 in a series called "Results of the Archbold Expeditions"—all subsidized by Dick Archbold and mostly published in the "Novitiates" series of the museum.
>
> This was possibly the first publication based on fieldwork at the Archbold station. A. L. Rand and Per Host had published a "Mammals of Highlands County, Florida," and Rand had published a little paper or two based on the months Archbold and he spent in Arizona before Archbold secured the Florida property.
>
> I was the only scientist at the station; both Rand and Per Host had left. Frank Rinald was not there either, but there was a bookkeeper that sometimes joined Archbold and me at lunch or dinner (Dick always took breakfast in his own quarters).

I didn't get to the station again until 1952 when Mrs. Amadon and I were there for a few days with our two daughters. In later years, my wife and I (without the daughters) were usually there for a month each winter. One of Dick Archbold's many generous traits was his willingness to have scientists bring their spouses, whenever there was room.

I was made a member of the advisory committee. When someone sent in an application for research at the station, copies would be sent to the committee for review. I once made the mistake of writing that a certain proposal "looked pretty thin to me." The Archbold secretary, then housed in the mammal department at the museum, told me that Mr. Archbold remarked, "It's my station, so I can invite whomever I please." Needless to say, I never made that mistake again!

Years later I was a member of the four-person "Science Advisory Committee" along with Professors Richard Root of Cornell, an ecologist, Jay Savage of the University of Miami, a herpetologist, and Michael Barbour of the University of California at Davis, a botanist. For years Professor Root would bring a class to Florida each winter and make its base at the Archbold station. That may have been after "Mr. A," as Prof[essor] Woolfenden called him, was no longer with us.

Aside from the researchers of its paid staff, the Archbold station has had several visiting professors who, often with graduate students and associates, returned to the station year after year carrying out major long-term research projects. Among them are Dr. Warren Abrahamson of Bucknell University on plant ecology, Dr. Thomas Eisner of Cornell on insect physiology, the author of this volume on the biology of the honey bee, and Professor Glen Woolfenden from the University of South Florida on the social dynamics of the Florida scrub jay. This bird is so tame that it can readily be handled and individually recognized. Further, its nesting habits are remarkable: the young of one year sometimes remain and help their parents rear the next year's brood of young. The studies of the cooperative breeding of this bird at the Archbold station are cited around the world in books and articles on bird behavior.

Mr. Archbold was always solicitous about the welfare of his help. When I was there in the spring of 1943, a humorous incident occurred. Once a week he would rent a movie and invite all the ground and machine shop crew, perhaps fifteen or twenty or more, including families, to see it in one of the labs. One night a screaming woman entered the darkened lab and practically dragged her man out bodily because he had "sinned" by attending the "motion pictures"!

Mr. Archbold always had his own workroom and office. He preferred things mechanical but would tackle any task that he thought was for the good of the station. Once he was cataloging some photographic slides of birds. I was working in the next lab. He came in and said, "Wha, wha, what is a Bachman's sparrow?" (Dick didn't stutter, but when he was excited, he sometimes had a little trouble getting started.) I said, "I think it's sometimes called the pine woods sparrow. Shall I come and we'll look in another book?" "No, no. I'll do it," and he dashed off. When I saw him a little later, with that boyish grin he never lost, he said emphatically, "You were right!"

In his later years, at least, I believe there were days when Dick never left the main building, which, of course, also contained his living quarters. He preferred to work in his lab and would never, for example, be encountered on the many woodland paths, which sometimes enticed others to "take a break." His daily attire was the simplest of brown shirts and khaki pants. If some morning he was "dressed up," it usually meant that he would soon depart for one of the board meetings of the Rural Electrification Administration.

Life at the Station as Described by Erik Tetens Nielson

Danish entomologist Erik Tetens Nielson had a special interest in migratory butterflies. He visited the United States to study these insects and, after meeting with several fellow entomologists, joined the group of visitors at the Archbold station. Archbold encouraged his research, and he worked at the station for several months. Later, he joined the staff at the Florida Medical Entomology Laboratory at Vero Beach, which is a University of Florida research center concerned with mosquitoes, biting midges, and related insect groups of public health importance. He remained there for the rest of his career.

In the fall of 1989, Nielson wrote some reminiscences about his days at the station. The enthusiasm of those who visited is apparent in the following unpublished vignette written by him and abridged by R. A. Morse.

In an idle moment during a stay in Lund (Sweden) I examined the notice-board and found there something about a place called Archbold Biological Station, which seemed to be ideal for the studies I intended. I wrote to them. The reply from Archbold said we (my wife and I) should be welcome. One of the first days in New Year 1949 we arrived in Florida.

We had heard about his expeditions to Madagascar and to New Guinea; how he had invented a new way to explore difficult country by keeping the members supported by air. That he had planned a new expedition, which had to be canceled by the outbreak of World War II. We heard the story about how he met a friend, Roebling, who wanted to dispose of a property at Lake Placid, Florida, and how he decided to convert Archbold Expeditions into a permanent station by acquiring the property—for one dollar—PLUS UPKEEP as Archbold himself added, when he told the story.

This was the man who received us at the railroad station in Sebring with the utmost kindness and drove us home to the place, which should become so dear to us, but at first left us in bewilderment. We were introduced to a number of people, and let me first tell about them.

There was Frank Rinald, who took care of the daily business of the station; he was also secretary, librarian and the man who could advise us about everything. Through American Museum, he had for many years been attached to Archbold Expeditions. He was married to an artist, who had made drawings for the museum. They and their little son lived in one of the most beautiful of the cottages belonging to the Station. Frank and Helen became our very good friends.

In another cottage lived Simeon Walter, who had been chauffeur for Archbold's father. He drove daily to Lake Placid and made the shopping for all who needed it. He took care of the cars of the Station. On the lawn in front of his house (cottage 1) there was a place for a croquet court and we had often a game there before dinner with [James G.] Needham and the [Sam P.] van der Kloots.

We were installed in the main building, and there was also, beside Archbold himself, the housekeeper, Mrs. Knott, and the mechanic, Bob Nagel. He was very clever, and a great asset for the Station. He spent a lot of time in building the beautiful ship model that still adorns the dining room. I think his best friends were the birds and the squirrels that he spoiled by means of expensive pecan nuts.

There were five or six local people to do the manual work; when not occupied with other work, they were growing vegetables, both for the household of Archbold and for the cottages. In addition to this, Archbold himself had hydroponic experiments that produced excellent vegetables, also to the households in the cottages. Nearly every week came a truck with oranges, beans, corn, cabbage or peas after the season.

Most beloved and honored of the guests was James G. Needham from Cornell University. He stayed most winters at the Station until he became too old to make the trip. He, as an entomologist and fresh-water biologist, had been the central point among the people who had made Cornell the center of entomology and the natural place for the international entomology congress in 1928. He was an inspiration to be with. He combined an old man's wisdom with the ready humor of a young man. His ability as a teacher was shown every time he had a guest in his laboratory. He always found some object on his table and told about it with such clarity and enthusiasm, that the guest always felt he was initiated in one of Nature's secrets.

But there were many other interesting people, the botanist Leonard J. Brass lived in one of the cottages at the Station when he was not out on expeditions. Other guests during this period were Krombein, Hartmann, Schneirla, Klots, Bogert and the Bowers. Especially the young van der Kloots became our good friends. Dr. van der Kloot, a botanist from Nova Scotia, made several trips to the Station studying the systematics of blueberries.

One of the first evenings I was working late in the laboratory as it is my custom; when I went upstairs to our room and would close the outer door, I could not find a key. The next morning I told Archbold that I was sorry that I had left the door unlocked to which he replied, "we never lock the doors here." The only exception was the door to the office, which had to be locked for insurance reasons. But the key was on a board over the door, the board was white-painted and many dirty hands had left their mark and showed clearly where the key was. For some reason it gave me a feeling of freedom to be at a place without suspicion, a wonderful feeling of belonging to the place.

It was wonderful to drive around in Florida and learn more and more about the butterflies, to become familiar with the country and the people, and best of all to come back to the Station. But we missed our two daughters and hoped we could get an extension to continue our work after the half year, which was far from being enough. Archbold had become interested in our work and when he heard of our difficulties, he suggested that we should stay a year more, get the girls over, move into one of the cottages and become members of the staff of this institute, which fitted me so perfectly. It was one of the best evenings in our lives.

It was not only the perfect beauty of the surroundings; it was not only the calm rhythm of the work that fitted me so well; it was, above all the personality of Archbold, which made everything so good. In one of the few confidential talks I had with him, he said, "I know that I am not a scientist, and what I make myself is nothing; but I hope, I am able to help other people to do some good science." I was too moved to say anything, but in that moment I came to think . . .

that everything he did, was to help other people, maybe . . . with the ultimate goal to help science, but really in every respect.

I thought of how little he did to enjoy himself. A couple of times every month he went bowling with Rinald. A couple of times he went over to Palm Beach to see his sister. And once every fall he went over to the west coast and went fishing with a friend for a couple of days. In the years I knew him, he had a beer with his lunch and a cocktail or two before dinner. In the evening, he came over to the cottages and spent the evening telling stories of his life (some of these stories he told several times). He went early to bed and I had plenty of working time after his visits.

Once . . . I [needed to] cut a piece of wood and went in next door and used the band saw. Some minutes later Archbold appeared, very excited: Had I used the band saw? He had heard the sound of it. I confessed and said that I had done so before in Denmark. But he was still angry and told me that I had to leave such things to his people. I was mad at him, but later I understood that it was just his care for me.

His care for other people was evident, although it only appeared in glimpses. There was shelter for people who lived in unreliable homes in case of hurricanes. The only fire engine was at the Station. One night when I was the only adult male at home, he asked me to come with him to a fire in the black town. When the school got a band, he provided uniforms for it; unfortunately it did not improve the sound of the music, but they looked at least impressive.

In some respects Archbold remained an enigma to us. We did not know how he had been before. We never learned why he suddenly fell half asleep, as when he drove us so masterfully in his car at high speed, 85–95 mph, he sometimes reduced the speed to 65–70 and seemed to be going to fall asleep, My wife, sitting between us, was always prepared to speak to him and wake him up in such cases. He was a lonely man, but he liked children and he had a sense of childish humor. Once he sneaked up behind me while I was measuring some difficult thing and every time I bent over the instrument, he shaded the light so I could not see anything. I enjoyed the joke and it was completely unnecessary for him to be ashamed of the joke.

Once van der Kloot wanted to try to play a clarinet and tried to hide efforts in the soundproof room. Archbold connected it to a couple of loud-speakers so the miserable sounds were broadcasted all over the Station.

Finally I will think on an evening at our cottage. We had a visit of a friend of mine from Denmark, Ole Vinding. He went as young man to France and married (the first of many times) a granddaughter of Renoir. Lived for many years as a reporter in Paris, came home to Denmark before the war and became the best interviewer of the Danish press. He wrote masterful books on the impressionists. We invited him to dinner with Archbold and Provost, my friend in mosquito research. We had the dinner out in the garden and remained there all the beautiful evening. I do not remember what we ate, but it was perfect, nor do I remember what we drank, but it was good. I do not even remember the many topics of our conversation, but I recall that it was so calm that we had candles on the table after it got dark.

I realize that the picture of Richard Archbold I am able to give is very incomplete; he should perhaps most be remembered as the explorer and for his expeditions. But his contemporary friends did not do it, and they are now gone. I hope with these lines to have him to be remembered as a most remarkable man, a noble and unselfish creator of good science.

Mirian Beck's Article on Archbold

The following article appeared in the *Lake Placid Journal* on August 5, 1976, shortly after Archbold's death. The author, Mirian Beck, wrote for the *Journal* and was a teacher of English at the Lake Placid High School. It explains in clear terms what people in the community thought of him.

Richard Archbold—A Legend

Lake Placid has lost a true friend and a good man with the passing of Richard Archbold.

Richard Archbold was, of course a legend locally and in the far corners of the earth. Stories abound around town of the tall, shy, lonely man with the piercing eyes and abrupt manner who had some mysterious connection with the fabulous Rockefeller family and equally fabulous connection with the American Museum of Natural History, who "talked with the animals" down on the great estate on Red Hill and who held court daily with visiting scientists from all over the world—the man whose efforts brought rural electrification to the remote ranches of Lake Placid and who drove his Cadillac through the sandy roads to read meters—who took delight in conducting the drawing of the Glades Electric members' meeting and of whom all those who had worked with him at the biological station he had set up spoke with affection and respect.

But there is another legend of Richard Archbold which belongs in the remote areas of New Guinea and Madagascar, and this has been recorded in the pages of *National Geographic Magazine,* the *Saturday Evening Post* and the *Natural History Magazine.* This was the story of the expeditions he financed, organized and led to the then unexplored regions of Madagascar and New Guinea. (When Nelson Rockefeller's son was lost there some 15 years ago, it was the Archbold maps that his friends used in their efforts to find him.)

For those of us who knew Richard Archbold over the years—even though remotely—it is hard to see him go, but the regret is mingled with gratitude and pride. Gratitude that he lifted the horizons of our little country town to include the whole world and pride that he chose to live in Lake Placid.

The Archbold Legacy

The Post-Archbold Years

Leonard J. Brass retired March 31, 1966, and James N. Layne (see appendix) joined the Lake Placid staff a little over a year later on June 1, 1967, as director of research. Upon Archbold's death in 1976, Layne became executive director of the station. Shortly before his death, Archbold changed his will so that the station was his sole beneficiary. This brought to an end support for an Archbold curator at the American Museum, though funding continued for about five years after his death.

The reassignment of moneys upon Archbold's death brought even more change, as witnessed by the growth of the station's annual and later the biennial reports. During Layne's tenure as executive director, the research staff grew and more attention was paid to education and conservation. Layne's accomplishments are outlined in the 1993–94 biennial report. Of special importance to those working at the station today is that several tracts of land, most notably Lake Annie and its environs, were acquired, so that the present contiguous holdings are about 5,000 acres.

The Buck Island Ranch

On November 30, 1988, Archbold Expeditions leased the Buck Island Ranch, approximately 10,000 acres and 17 miles square, from the John D. and Catherine T. MacArthur Foundation for a period of thirty years for one dollar. The foundation gave to this organization, as an outright grant, the 1,500 to 2,000 breeding cattle and the machinery on the ranch—a gift valued at approximately $2 million—as well as the nearly full crop of ripe citrus in the ranch's 170-acre grove.

The ranch lies south of Route 70 about eight miles east of the station property and was already being used by some station personnel, most notably James N. Layne. The long-range research goal is to study the interrelationships of cattle ranching, citrus production, and the native ecological systems of south-central Florida. The lease called for continuing the cattle ranching on the 4,728 acres of improved pasture, mostly bahia grass, and 5,096 acres of native areas that contain a mixture of wetland and slough vegetation. The Harney Pond Canal, constructed by the U.S. Corps of Engineers, runs through the property.

In 1991, the University of Florida (the Institute of Food and Agricultural Sciences) and Archbold Biological Station, aided by a grant from the Frank "Sonny" Williamson Cattle Company, each committed funds for agro-ecological studies on the ranch. The concerns of the South Florida Water Management District regarding the deposition of cow fecal matter and phosphorus and the movement of this nutrient-rich water into the canal and Lake Okeechobee are being addressed, among other things.

Background on the lease and goals of the initiatives are contained in two printed documents, *Buck Island Ranch Research Initiative* (two pages, undated, circa 1992) and *A Proposal to the John D and Catherine*

T. MacArthur Foundation drafted by James N. Layne and James L. Wolfe, executive director (twenty-nine pages, undated, circa 1986), both in the station archives. Further details concerning the lease and the ranch are found in the forty-seventh annual report of Archbold Biological Station of Archbold Expeditions for 1988.

The Library

The library at the Archbold Biological Station was founded at the same time the station was acquired in 1941. Today, it is the second best biologically oriented library in Florida (after that of the University of Florida at Gainesville). Its nucleus was Archbold's personal collection from his office at the American Museum of Natural History. The library is a noncirculating research collection. Interlibrary loans are available.

The library today has about 5,500 books and 5,500 bound periodical volumes. It has approximately 300 serials and is currently receiving about 250 paid and free subscriptions ranging from *Science* and *Nature* to local Florida journal series. The rare book collection is modest and contains about 75 titles. There are around 12,000 cataloged slides in the natural history collection. The picture collection includes about 1,000 photographs. The archives comprise approximately 17,000 reprints, correspondence, clippings, manuscripts, and memorabilia from the Archbold expeditions. There is a large collection of government documents from the U.S. Department of Agriculture, especially the Forest Service, and the Interior Department as pertains to the Fish and Wildlife Service. Publications from the Smithsonian Institution are also well represented. There have been a number of important donations from visiting scientists and the staff.

The Collections

It is difficult to say precisely how many species of plants, animals, and microbes exist, but they number in the millions. This diversity of species is well understood by biologists who work with plant and animals, and Archbold was aware of the impact of this great number of living things on our lives. Equally important, he understood the importance of collecting and properly labeling specimens so that investigators had a record of what was present in a given area. Throughout his career he encouraged those who visited and collected at the station, whatever their interest, to leave a synoptic collection of the plants and animals that were of particular interest to them. As a result, as they come and go, investigators are able to examine the Archbold plant and animal collections and in this manner gain immediate knowledge of the local flora and fauna.

The plant and animal collections at the Archbold Biological Station are research collections and are not on public view except under special circumstances and/or by appointment. It is a special art to collect, prepare, and maintain plant and animal specimens so they will be available for future generations of scientists. The specimens must be kept under temperature and humidity conditions that favor their preservation.

The Insect Collection

The insect collection, which has been growing since the founding of the station, has over 50,000 specimens. Most of these are mounted on specially designed pins, though some are preserved in vials and bottles in alcohol. Like specimens collected in any biological regimen, they all have labels that include information about when, where, and who was responsible for their collection. This information is necessary for those who are interested in studying a particular group. Some groups of insects are better represented than others, which reflects the interests of the researchers who have worked at the station. There are, for example, specimens of all the 112 species of ants found on the property. More species of ants have been found there than in any other known site in North America because this location is characterized by a complex association of Florida highlands and lowlands. The ant collection also reflects the special interests of the resident entomologist, Mark Deyrup.

Not only did Archbold encourage collecting, but he had his own printing press and delighted in printing labels on high-quality, archival paper for visiting entomologists. His press used a small type size so that each label could provide many facts yet occupy minimal space on an insect pin. The insect collection is the second best in Florida, following that of the Florida State Department of Agriculture in Gainesville.

The Bird Collection

About 470 species of birds have been recorded from Florida. Many of them are common and well-known, but many are seen rarely and are little known. Also to be found in Florida are many species of exotics transported to the state by humans.

Like the insect collection, the Archbold bird collection is the second best in Florida after that at Gainesville. The bird collection consists of about 1,400 study skins representing 75 percent of the naturally occurring species known from the state and a sampling of exotics. Series, that is, many specimens of a single species, are kept for only a few species that are of current research interest. The collection also includes about 500 bird skeletons and 100 egg sets. It has been largely built up by longtime Archbold research associate Glen E. Woolfenden, who together with his students has a special interest in the endangered Florida scrub jay.

The Herbarium

The station holds an estimated 3,600 specimens of vascular plants, of which nearly 600 represent the plants that may be found on the station grounds. Between one third to a half of the specimens were collected between 1945 and 1965 by Leonard Brass, the resident botanist during

A researcher examines the nest cavity of a red-cockaded woodpecker as part of a long-range demographic study of this species in south-central Florida. These birds have declined with the loss of old-growth pine forests. Various research projects examine the viability of populations occurring in remnant and fragmented forests. Photo by R. Bowman.

Much of Florida's xeric oak scrubs have given way to human residential development. More than 30 percent of the extant Florida scrub jays occur in residential areas, and research focuses on the impact of increasing urbanization on the jays. Finding nests and monitoring reproductive success and subsequent survival of young birds are integral parts of this research. Photo by R. Bowman.

that time. Brass's specimens are of special value because of the ecological data he included with each item. Additions to the plant collection have been made by Dr. Eric Menges, the current resident botanist and research biologist, who is actively preparing a computer database of the plant holdings that may be used by researchers interested in certain plant groups.

The Vertebrate Collection

The station has an extensive collection of mammals, reptiles, amphibians, and fishes. (The bird collection is separate and has already been discussed.) The last three are preserved in 70 percent alcohol, while most of the mammals are preserved as round or flat skins. Skeletons accompany many of the mammal skins, and thousands of soft parts, stomachs, livers, and so forth, are also preserved for diagnosis as the need arises. The collection has representative samples of those vertebrates found on the station as well those from the rest of Florida that may be of value in comparative studies.

In the early days, as the station grew, miscellaneous vertebrates were collected, but it was not until James N. Layne joined the station staff as research director that the building of an extensive vertebrate collection was taken seriously. In addition to the station collection of about 300 round and flat skins, over 7,000 mammal specimens and 1,000 reptile specimens were sent to the American Museum of Natural History in New York City. As with the insect and other collections, many of the labels in the vertebrate collection were printed by Archbold.

Current Staff and Visitors

The number of staff varies but at present (1999) includes approximately seventeen full and part-time researchers, six research associates, an office staff of six, a maintenance staff of four, and a housekeeping staff of three at the station proper. Among the researchers are the executive

Researchers measuring acorn production in the Florida scrub jay demography tract. Photo by G. Woolfenden.

director, who is also a research biologist, two full-time research biologists at the station and one at the MacArthur Agro-ecology Research Center, a librarian/information manager, an education coordinator, a geographic information systems officer, a land manager, and a computer systems manager. The remainder of the research staff are supported by grant funds or with part-time appointments.

Professors G. E. Woolfenden and J. W. Fitzpatrick with a Florida scrub jay, the state's only endemic bird species. Photo by G. Woolfenden.

Father, mother, and second helper Florida scrub jays tend two nestlings. (A helper is a youngster who helps its parents feed and care for their young.) Photo by G. Woolfenden.

Numerous species of butterflies, including the gulf fritillary, the cloudless sulfur, and the long-tailed skipper, migrate down the Florida peninsula for the winter. These directional insect traps were used by researchers from the University of Florida to determine whether the Archbold Biological Station is a way station or an endpoint of these migrations.(The station is, in fact, a wintering destination.) Photo by N. Deyrup

Lake Annie, an undeveloped ninety-acre sinkhole lake typical of those in south-central Florida. Photo by R. Morse.

A swarm of honey bees orients to their queen because of the pheromones she produces, and may be led by exposing her to them. Photo by R. Morse.

Examination of the 1993–94 and 1995–96 biennial reports shows that during each of these two-year periods, over forty-five interns and graduate students worked at the station. Several of the graduate students did thesis research. During that time about forty public and private school groups toured the station each year, and more than six workshops were held annually. The facilities at the station were used by over eighty visiting scientists from nearly twenty colleges, five museums, and seven government agencies during the last two years. Use of the station was acknowledged in over a dozen articles published by these persons each year. There were forty articles authored or coauthored by station staff each year. More than 150 college students participated in formal classes held at the station or as part of a group touring it each year.

Housing and Facilities for Guests

The Archbold Biological Station offers several types of accommodations for visitors, ranging from dormitory-style rooms, to main house rooms, to cottages. The seven cottages are different from each other. They have one or two bedrooms. Each is stocked with basic kitchen necessities, linens, and cleaning equipment. All main house and dormitory rooms and cottages are climate controlled. Meals are available six days a week for anyone in any of these accommodations.

A laboratory room forty by thirty feet is set aside for visitors. Additionally, there are several flight cages and other small buildings that may be used for research. Several types of vehicles, including cars, small trucks, all-terrain vehicles, and boats, are also available for use. The facilities include a 100-seat auditorium, a conference room, and darkroom.

Public Service

The Rural Electrification Administration
and the Glades Electrical Cooperative

From 1945 until his death, Richard Archbold was involved in the formation and management of the Glades Electrical Cooperative, which
was founded under federal guidelines. The cooperative is a member-
owned, nonprofit organization that provides electrical power to Glades
and parts of Hendry, Highlands, and Okeechobee counties. In 1997, it
reported it had 13,000 members, over 1,950 miles of power lines, and
fifty-four employees, with headquarters in Moore Haven (the Glades
County seat).

The federal executive order founding the Rural Electrification Administration (REA) was signed by President Franklin D. Roosevelt on
May 11, 1935. The objective was to bring to rural Americans the same
benefits from the use of electricity that were enjoyed by urban people.
The legislation formally creating the administration was approved on

May 20, 1936. Details concerning the REA are documented in the paperback publication *Rural Electrification Act of 1936 with Amendments as Approved through Dec. 17, 1993*, available from the REA in Washington.

When Richard Archbold arrived at what was to become the Archbold Biological Station in 1941, he found an on-site electrical generator, which was the sole power source. The generator ran by day, providing power only at that time and also charging the batteries that provided the station with power by night. The original, two-room building (a separate room was used for the large storage batteries) still stands, but the generator is now a diesel-driven affair that is used in emergencies only.

According to the late Ralph V. Wadlow of Palmdale, in central Glades County, who was a beekeeper acquaintance of the author's, even REA did not want to electrify Glades County and the surrounding environs because there were so few people scattered over such a great expanse of land. Wadlow served as the first secretary-treasurer of the Glades Electrical Cooperative. Wadlow said local people went to Archbold for help and that he responded by prodding the federal government into providing the needed assistance to form the Glades Electrical Cooperative. As a result, Archbold became a local hero. The Washington REA people had paid no attention to requests for information from the Glades County area residents, but he spoke with a more authoritative voice. According to the minutes of the first meeting of the board of trustees in January 1945, the 170 persons dependent upon the city of Moore Haven municipal electrical plant were also anxious to join the new cooperative as their plant needed repair and upgrading.

At that January 1945 meeting, Richard Archbold was elected a member of the board of trustees. He was elected vice president of the Glades Electrical Cooperative in July 1945 and president at the annual meeting in January 1947. He continued in that office until January 1956, when he was again elected vice president, an office he held until his death. He faithfully attended board meetings, and there were stories that he even served as a volunteer meter reader in the early days, when things were getting started. Until recently, the plaza at the station was often a repository for poles, wire, and even cooperative trucks, all indicative of his desire to enter into community affairs and to be of service.

According to Bass et al. (1985), Moore Haven had an electrical generating plant and a "forty-ton ice house" that was built in 1915. However, the rest of the county was without electricity. Presumably the plant was lost in the hurricane-flood in Moore Haven on September 18, 1926. The hurricane came with winds up to 160 miles per hour, and, without any warning, ten feet of water from Lake Okeechobee flowed in the streets of the city. Hundreds of people died, and bodies continued to be found in the glades for months afterward. Moore Haven was under martial law, and the National Guard was placed in charge. The city was slow to recover. The Herbert Hoover Dike was built around the southern end of the lake in the early 1930s by the Army Corps of Engineers.

The activities leading to the formation of the Glades Electrical Cooperative are also recorded by Bass et al. (1985). In January 1945 the first signed applications for membership in the cooperative were received, and the first annual meeting was held. In attendance at the meeting were two officials from REA, who explained the way in which a cooperative could be formed and how REA would assist in loaning money. The area to be served was smaller than is serviced today and included all of Glades County, part of Hendry, and that part of Highlands County south of Route 70. The fact that these officials offered advice just a few months shy of ten years after REA had come into existence testifies to the foot-dragging done by REA in electrifying the area.

The first loan to the cooperative was granted in July 1945. This included moneys to build a generating plant in Moore Haven and to construct the first power lines. However, it was not until June of 1946 that money was borrowed to extend the lines into Highlands County and to the Archbold Station in January 1947.

At the time of this writing, all public service companies and cooperatives in the United States that provide electric and/or natural gas to local citizens are undergoing deregulation and will be subject to competition. There has been much discussion at recent meetings of the cooperative about the changes this will bring, but at this time no one has been able to predict what will happen with any degree of accuracy.

The Corkscrew Swamp Sanctuary

Richard Archbold gave ongoing support to the preservation of native lands and habitats. For example, his annual report to the American Museum dated June 22, 1955, states that he and Brass collaborated with the Corkscrew Cypress Rookery Association and The Nature Conservancy to preserve an additional seven square miles of virgin cypress swamp and adjoining buffer land for that preserve. This preserve, in Collier County, is formally known as the Corkscrew Swamp Sanctuary of the National Audubon Society.

The Weather Station

The National Weather Service depends on volunteers to operate the weather stations around the United States. The service provides equipment, but all other costs are born by the operators. There has been a weather station at the Archbold Biological Station since 1932. It became an official weather station in 1969 when it was moved from the shores of Lake June to its present location behind the tractor barn and north of the water tower.

Weather data was recorded at the station from 1932 through 1941 under the direction of resident engineer Alexander Blair. (Data for a few months in 1941 are missing.) In the beginning a record was made of the rainfall and maximum and minimum temperatures. Blair added data on humidity, barometric pressure, and wind speed in 1934. The equipment for registering wind speed was kept on top of the water tower for several years, but several lightning hits made it necessary to move it to ground level. Additional equipment was added to measure relative humidity (1969), soil temperature at three depths (1970), evaporation with associated anemometers, evaporation pan water temperatures, solar radiation (1980), and wind speed and direction and barometric pressure (1982).

Civic Activities

Richard Archbold worked with a number of Lake Placid groups for the betterment of the community. Some of these activities are mentioned in the station annual reports.

During World War II, he was active with the Federal Civil Defense and was awarded a certificate for taking a course in administration in its staff college in Miami. In 1958, he was elected president of the Lake Placid Lions Club, of which he was a founding and active member for over ten years. He was secretary of the advisory council of Highlands Hammock State Park (1956–76), a member of the Florida State Museum Council (1956–70), chairman of the Highlands District American National Red Cross (1957–58) for two years and a director for six years, and chairman of the Lake Placid Boy Scout Troop Committee (1957).

The annual report for 1960–61 states that the station "was used as a place of shelter for 73 people" (including 33 Seminole Indians) during Hurricane Donna on September 10–11, 1960. This was a joint effort of the station and the American Red Cross, but the report also states that the station had served as a shelter in other years as well.

Memberships and Awards

Richard Archbold joined the Explorer's Club in 1929. He was appointed a research associate in the mammal department of the American Museum in 1932 following the successful Madagascar expedition. He was elected a member of the Institute of Aeronautical Sciences and given a special certificate of award for his contributions during the New Guinea expeditions (1940). He was a "Decorated Officer Order Orange Nassau" (The Netherlands) for his exploration of the Dutch portion of New Guinea (1940). He was elected a life member of the American Society of Mammalogists for his contributions to the field. He was elected a fellow of the American Association for the Advancement of Science (1960), a member of the Australian Mammal Society (1961),

Richard Archbold at the station. Station archives.

and an endowment member of the American Museum of Natural History (1968). Archbold was awarded the Conservation Achievement Award from the Florida Conservation Council (1974).

Some Plants and Animals Named in Honor of Richard Archbold[11]

As with many scientific patrons before him, Richard Archbold's name lives on in the scientific nomenclature of numerous plant and animal species that bear his name as an accolade for his support of science and scientists. A typical comment that is recorded with the description of the plant or animal is that of Wirth (1994), who named a sand fly after Archbold: "This species is named in honor of Richard Archbold, founder of the Archbold Biological Station. The Station has been my host for several periods of productive ceratopogonid research."

The following list is not complete. Even as I write, more species are being described honoring Richard Archbold.

Animals

Accipiter nanus (archboldi) Stresemann, Selawesi dwarf sparrow-hawk

Aegotheles [albertisi] archboldi Rand, Archbold's owlet nightjar

Archboldia papuensis Rand, Archbold's bower bird

Dacelo tyro archboldi Rand, Aru giant kingfisher

Eurostopodus archboldi Mayr & Rand, Archbold's nightjar

Petroica archboldi Rand, the rock robin-flycatcher

Newtonia archboldi Delacour & Berlioz, Archbold's newtonia

Archboldomys luzonensis Musser, Mount Isarog shrew rat

Admestina archboldi Piel, a jumping spider

Geolycosa xera archboldi McCrone, a burrowing wolf spider

Tekellina archboldi Levi, a theridiid spider

Ansyndetus archboldi Deyrup, a long-legged fly

Archboldargia mirifica Lieftinck, a New Guinea damselfly

Atrichopogon archboldi Wirth, a sand fly
Barichneumon archboldi Heinrich, an ichneumon wasp
Chrysis archboldi Kimsey, a cuckoo wasp
Dasymutilla archboldi Schmidt & Mickel, a velvet ant
Eumayriella archboldi Melika & Abrahamson, a cynipid gall wasp
Formica archboldi Smith, an ant
Lanthusa richardi Lieftinck, a dragonfly
Liriomyza archboldi Frost, a leaf miner
Minilimosina archboldi Marshall, a sphaerocerid fly
Neotridactylus archboldi Deyrup & Eisner, a pigmy mole cricket
Neuroterus archboldi Melida & Abrahamsen, a gall wasp
Photomorphus archboldi Manley & Deyrup, a velvet ant
Selonodon archboldi Galley, a beetle
Smithistruma archboldi Deyrup & Cover, a dacetine ant
Telamona archboldi Froeschner, a tree hopper
Tripoxylon tridentatum archboldi Krombein, a larrid wasp

Plants

Aceratium Archboldianum Smith
Carpodetus Archboldianus Reeder
Elaeocarpus Archboldianus Smith

Richard Archbold's Living Legacy, 1976–1998

FRANCES ARCHBOLD HUFTY

It would seem that my brother Richard Archbold's great purpose in life was that of facilitator. Throughout his life he was, more or less, devoted to science and scientists, genuinely interested in understanding how the natural world works. In the early years his share of the family's wealth furnished the significant funds needed to move field biologists and their vast amounts of equipment around the globe. Incurring large expenses, he supplied the various vehicles, airplanes, boats, and other means of supporting transportation. Almost unobtrusively, he arranged for administrative support; business concerns—finances, investments, insurance, and the like—were areas in which he consulted with the family.

When it came to setting up the Archbold Biological Station, Dick seemed to have a vision of what he wanted from the outset. In the early years there was a lot of work consolidating and publishing much of the earlier expedition material. But as time progressed, the station's facilities were built up under his aegis to accommodate on-site visiting investigators. He always took great pleasure in playing his part in these scientific endeavors—enthusiastically saying "I can do *that*," as he would tackle the design and fabrication of some tool or piece of experimental equipment. I have fond memories of Dick constructing the most fantastic of scientific gadgets, such as a huge truck with a blazing array of four powerful three-foot-diameter lights with a "trip" for night photography. What pleased him more than anything else was the growing catalog of research going on. With evident pleasure, he hosted many of the world's greatest ecologists at his dining table. Around the station he acquired critical additional acres of Florida scrub habitat, harboring some of the rarest species in North America. He invited the highest-caliber guardians of ecological research to be the station's resident biologists. Unlike many of the notable philanthropists of the twentieth century, he personally lived out his philanthropic intent. And we, his family, looked in from the outside with curiosity at "Uncle Dick," master of his own "little kingdom" out there in the back of beyond, in the Florida scrub.

The latter half of his private and personal life, sheltered with scientists and the scrub, continued unsullied until spring 1976. Then, faced with the sudden onslaught of terminal pancreatic cancer, he lay in the hospital in Palm Beach, contemplating the fate of the station and all that he had worked toward. The family chatted quietly on the shaded balcony outside his hospital room, talking over his options, and whether we could play a role. Dick seemed surprised to realize that I, Frances, always the little sister, and certainly not a trained scientist, was actually quite curious about what he did and was willing to play a part in the future affairs of the station. Although, to him, I was probably still the "horse crazy" young girl of his youth, he seemed to appreciate my sympathy for, and my interest in, plants and animals. After all, ever since those earliest days in Thomasville, my heart has always been with nature. Anyway, in the midst of this quiet family discussion about his will,

Dick suddenly leaped up from his sickbed and shouted out, "Typing, typing, I can do *that!*" And so he proceeded, with firmness of thought, to type up the provisions of his will. He decided, then and there, to set aside his personal fortune, in funds to be administered by a board of trustees, to provide for the future scientific activities of the station. It is remarkable how this sum of money, certainly significant, but nothing in comparison to the vast sums spent by government agencies, has provided for so much research over the years. His words set the stage for a living legacy of his lifetime's interests—a legacy that grows and binds, like a braided vine, tying and coupling his beloved station and its surrounds, its scientists and, quite definitely, our family.

It all started at our first board meeting on August 4, 1976, the night after his funeral at the station. I took over the role of president, and Page, my husband, took over the responsibilities of treasurer and secretary. For several years our family held the board meetings on Christmas Day at the station, accompanied by plum puddings with flaming brandy. Page thought this would be the least intrusive in terms of his other work and financial responsibilities, although, in hindsight, it must have been quite a strain on the staff. We now meet at the station once a year, usually around Thanksgiving. All of my five children, Dick's nephew and nieces—Jack, Alexandra, Archie, Page-Lee, and Mary—have served at various times on the board of trustees. Their families too have joined in our purpose, and, to my great delight, our board of trustees now includes some of my grandchildren, with more in the wings for the future.

As intended, by setting aside his personal share of the family wealth, Dick was able to further the scope and scale of scientific activities at the station and beyond. As the result of his support for research, the name Archbold now stands for high-quality ecological research throughout the world. All these research activities are, of course, well documented in the annual and biennial reports published by the station. It is amazing to consider how far we, as a family board of trustees, have grown in our knowledge and understanding of these scientific works. My own regular trips out to the station, usually every Thursday, are always opportunistic, serendipitous, and invariably interesting; a great source of pleasure and fascination to me over the past twenty-two years.

Under the guidance of Jim Layne, Dick's choice as executive director (who served in this role from 1976 to 1985), the board endorsed the use of the endowment funds to emphasize long-term ecological research, something that government funding has rarely fostered. Layne's various long-term studies on small mammals, birds, and vegetative changes established Archbold as a field station par excellence in Florida. Annual transfers from the Archbold endowment supported numerous interesting studies at the station. Anyone who has had the pleasure of a field trip with Glen Woolfenden or John Fitzpatrick is invariably enthralled with the friendly antics of their study species, the scrub jay, bouncing from your hands to your head, and usually begging for peanuts to bury in the sand. Equally fascinating is how these two scientists (Woolfenden started the study in 1969) have painstakingly documented the lives of every member of every scrub jay family; regular monthly efforts repeated year in and year out. In doing so they have generated extraordinarily fruitful data, which has become one of the world's classic studies of the factors governing an individual animal's behavior.

Mark Deyrup, Archbold entomologist and everyone's favorite natural history storyteller, is easily tempted to lead us off into the scrub, revealing extraordinary details about the lives of insects and plants in this complex landscape. Leaping pygmy mole crickets that graze on subterranean algal meadows. So many different species of ants (112, but changing) that live at the station, apparently in a world of life-threatening raindrops, resin balls, and shifting sands. Deyrup has continued Dick's interest in species collections, caring for vast cabinets storing rank upon rank of pinned insects—apparently one of the best collections at any field station, with nearly 4,500 species.

Tom Eisner, eminent Cornell biologist who first came to the station in 1960, has shared with us his almost unbelievable accounts of the ferocious chemical arsenals employed by plants and animals to attract mates, or repel enemies, or defend their offspring. Recently I coerced my friends to join me in these scrub expeditions. Members of the Palm Beach Garden Club have stoically marched with me in the wake of Eric Menges, prominent station plant ecologist, to help, as rather lowly assistants, in his studies of the lives of the rare plants of the Florida scrub. It is another world to us, so removed from the showy grandeur of cultivated gardens, but really so beautiful and engaging when you take the time to get down to ground level.

Perhaps hardest to gauge is the influence of the station on generations of young biologists. Perhaps one of Dick's greatest living legacies is to have provided the facilities for a vast and ever expanding lineage of students, research assistants, and new faculty—all involved, at some stage, in ecological work at the station. They tell us they draw heavily on these station experiences as they teach and conduct research at many other colleges, universities, and scientific organizations throughout the world. Happily, many return for repeated visits.

Dick was concerned throughout his life about the loss of species and natural habitats; his reminiscing notes from the Madagascar trip show he was appalled, even then, at the rate of habitat destruction on this island of extraordinary diversity. He certainly loved the wilderness aspects of the station; I think its remoteness and isolation were among the reasons he was attracted to the property in the first place. His arguments in an advisory board meeting in 1944 concerning the value of the habitats of the station showed he had an interest in scrub early on. His enthusiasm for the scrub has been fully vindicated—the station now supports nineteen federally listed threatened and endangered species, including thirteen endemic plants associated with the Florida scrub.

After considerable thought and discussion, he expanded the boundaries of the station in 1973 and bought neighboring private lands within the three sections to the west of the railroad line. All this leads us to believe that he would have been a strong supporter of our continued program of land acquisition at the station. We have acquired over 1,500 acres since 1976, including Lake Annie in 1983 and a number of additional tracts throughout the late 1980s and 1990s. These local acquisitions are in line with the station's broader role, vigorously led by John Fitzpatrick, popular executive director from 1987 to 1995, to successfully promote conservation and public acquisition of scrub throughout Florida. It would be fair to say that protection of the critically threatened Lake Wales Ridge scrubs would not have become such a prominent flagship of Florida conservation without Dick's legacy of support for station research and conservation initiatives.

This legacy of support also enabled another remarkable change in understanding habitat requirements for the Florida scrub: the recognition of the need for fire to maintain scrub habitats. Ironically, Dick's consuming interest in wildfires at the station was in an era when the entire focus was on fire *suppression*. He armed the station with an array of gleaming fire engines, most notably "Big Red," a 1956 International Harvester that is still running and functional. No doubt he would have embraced, with gusto, the recent research showing fire is an essential process in the scrub. Our fire management plan for the station now calls for prescribed burns and accommodates lightning-induced fires when feasible; a 180° change from the earlier policies of fire suppression. I am sure he would have been delighted to join the action at the forefront—lighting a headfire—in the modern era of large-scale prescribed fire.

The other major change at the station occurred in 1988, when we took over operations at a 10,300-acre commercial cattle ranch—the MacArthur Agro-ecology Research Center—leased from the MacArthur Foundation for the princely sum of one dollar per year. This site, located fifteen miles east of the main property, on the wetland soils off the Lake Wales Ridge, had been used earlier by station scientists such as Jim

Layne for studies of the Florida caracara and the sandhill crane. The goal of the research programs at the ranch is to understand the relationship between ecological patterns and processes, and economic factors, in a working cattle ranch landscape. Our family has been involved in many agricultural enterprises, and we are intrigued by the thought of facilitating understanding of what it takes to have both economic and ecologically sustainable agriculture. I do not know exactly what Dick would have thought of this venture, but he was always very good at taking up "new things." The ranch seems a world away from the scrub, but not one that was unfamiliar to him. After all, he had originally promoted the station as a base from which to explore the pine flatwoods, hardwood and cabbage palm hammocks, dry prairies, wet prairies, freshwater swamps, streams, canals, lakes, and bay-gall and cypress swamps of this region, such as nearby Parker Island, which now, unfortunately, is no more. At the ranch, his legacy, and the philanthropic contributions of John D. MacArthur, jointly provide for this innovative and highly respected agro-ecology research venture.

As I end this book about my brother, I reflect on his lifetime of achievements, and all the pleasure he got out of playing his part in the scientific process. Equally important, I contemplate his thriving living legacy, poised for success into the next century and beyond. I doubt whether Dick considered the full ramifications of his family's involvement in the execution of his will. His trust in me, as family steward of his life's work, has had a profound influence on my own life and the lives of both my children and my grandchildren. Over the years we have all been seduced by the scientists' tales of fascinating scrub plants and animals, and so, gradually, we have learned the ways of the scrub—an acquired taste for us nonbiologists. Dick's endowment, under the oversight of the board, has grown significantly and is financially sound, servicing many of the funding needs of the station. This funding, in conjunction with our evolving partnership with these wonderful scientists and their intriguing projects, has further enhanced the station's reputation as a great hub of scientific thought and action. The active success of the Stations' mission— "dedicated to long-term ecological research and conservation. The primary focus is on the organisms and environments of the Lake Wales Ridge and adjacent central Florida. The Station's program is part of the global effort to understand, interpret, and preserve the earth's natural diversity"—is vigorous proof that Dick made the right decisions for his life and its legacy. In the end Richard Archbold, the great facilitator, let us all achieve success by allowing us to do the things we like.

Appendix

Leonard J. Brass

Leonard J. Brass (1900–1971) joined the first Archbold expedition to New Guinea in 1933 and, except for service in the Canadian army during World War II, served with Archbold and the American Museum of Natural History until his retirement in 1966. Brass wrote the article for *Science* magazine in 1944 that served as the model for the station as it is today. He became a naturalized citizen of the United States in 1947 and received an honorary doctorate from Florida State University in Tallahassee in 1962.

Brass was born and raised in Queensland, Australia, where he trained at the Queensland Herbarium. His first collecting expedition was to British New Guinea for the Arnold Arboretum of Harvard University in 1925–26. He was in charge of a second Arnold Arboretum expedition to the Solomon Islands in 1932–33. It was the experience with these two projects that led to his being recommended to Archbold.

During 1946 Brass accompanied an expedition to Vernay Nyasaland as botanist. In 1949–50 he was director of field operations for an Upjohn-Penick expedition to search tropical Africa for precursors for the manufacture of cortisone, a hormone used in medicine for sundry purposes. He led the fourth, fifth, and sixth Archbold expeditions, to the Cape York area of Australia (1947–48), the outlying islands of New Guinea (1956–57), and the central highlands of New Guinea (1958–59), respectively. In Florida, he was active with Archbold in establishing the Corkscrew Swamp Sanctuary and several other conservation projects.

Over the years Brass kept in close contact with the Arnold Arboretum and Harvard University, where he was appointed a collaborator on a joint botanical study of part of Florida. He was an adviser to a three-year study by the Arnold Arboretum to search for medicinal plants in the western Pacific, and served on a National Science Foundation panel on the merits of a botanical study of the Indian Ocean Islands.

Brass was a lucid and thorough writer on behalf of Archbold Expeditions. He had a talent for portraying to the popular press the aspects of the expeditions that the public would find most interesting. Most important, he was a strong and loyal supporter of the ideas that led to the formation of the station.

Austin L. Rand

Austin L. Rand (1905–82) was a close personal friend of Archbold's from the time they first met in 1929, when they were on the Madagascar expedition, until Archbold's death. Rand probably had a greater influence on Archbold's career than any other single individual. It was with Rand that Archbold developed his program to support the second and third New Guinea expeditions by air.

Rand was born and raised in rural Nova Scotia, where he was an avid hunter and outdoorsman and developed his interest in ornithology. He attended Acadia University, graduating in 1927. This institution awarded him an honorary D.Sc. degree in 1961. Rand moved from Acadia University to Cornell as a graduate student under the world's best-known North American ornithologist of his time, Arthur A. Allen.

Allen recommended that Rand become the replacement ornithologist on the Madagascar expedition when C. G. Harrold was fatally stricken with meningitis only days before the U.S. contingent was to leave New York. His Madagascar bird studies became his Ph.D. dissertation and a published book.

During the three New Guinea expeditions in the 1930s, Rand was co-leader and often point man as the expeditions proceeded. His writing skills became apparent at the time of his thesis writing and were put to good use in the preparation of the reports on the expeditions in the South Pacific.

When plans for a fourth expedition to New Guinea had to be scrapped because of the war, Rand accompanied Archbold on an expedition to Arizona. He next aided Archbold in taking control of the station property in 1941. Rand was a Canadian citizen and at the outset of World War II, out of loyalty to his country, returned to Canada and Ottawa, where he was first assistant zoologist and then associate zoologist in the National Museum of Canada. He later became acting chief of the biology division.

In 1947 Rand moved to Chicago as curator of ornithology at the Field Museum of Natural History and then served as chief curator of zoology, a position he held until his retirement. During this time he continued to be a prolific writer of both popular and technical articles and also wrote four books. Rand and his wife were regular contributors to the Chicago newspapers, and selections from their writing were compiled into the book *A Midwestern Almanac, Pageant of the Seasons.* He was a fellow in the American Ornithologists' Union and was its president from 1962 through 1964. Upon retirement to Lake Placid, the Rands continued to believe that it was important for scientists to make their knowledge available to the public, and wrote a weekly column, *Nature Notes,* for the *Lake Placid Journal.* In retirement he had a desk at the station and was there frequently.

In 1996 one of the original Roebling buildings on the station property was remodeled to house the bird collections and the administrative staff. The building was named in honor of Austin L. Rand.

James N. Layne (1926–)

In his early years, Layne was committed to ornithology, but after enrolling at Cornell University as an undergraduate he took courses on fishes and mammals, which changed the direction of his career. After earning his Ph.D. at Cornell under the direction of the well-known professor of mammalogy William J. Hamilton, Jr., he served on the faculties of Southern Illinois University in Carbondale and the University of Florida in Gainesville. In 1963 he returned to Cornell, where he taught for four years before becoming director of research at the Archbold Biological Station in 1967 with a concurrent appointment as Archbold curator of mammals at the American Museum. Prior to joining the station staff he had been a frequent visitor and researcher at the station. From 1976 to 1985 he was executive director of the station. He was president of the American Society of Mammalogists in 1970–72. He has served on a number of boards of environmental organizations and has worked closely with the Florida Game and Fresh Water Fish Commission and the U.S. Fish and Wildlife Service. His studies have been concerned with all aspects of conservation and wildlife ecology with a special interest in mammals and birds.

Layne was the 1995 Florida Academy of Sciences medallist. This annual award is given to a person who has made outstanding contributions to the "promotion of scientific research, to the stimulation of interest in the sciences, or to the diffusion of scientific knowledge." A colleague wrote that Layne "represents the best qualities of a Florida scientist—dedication, hard work, giving of one's self unselfishly for the benefit of others, sharing expertise and wisdom."

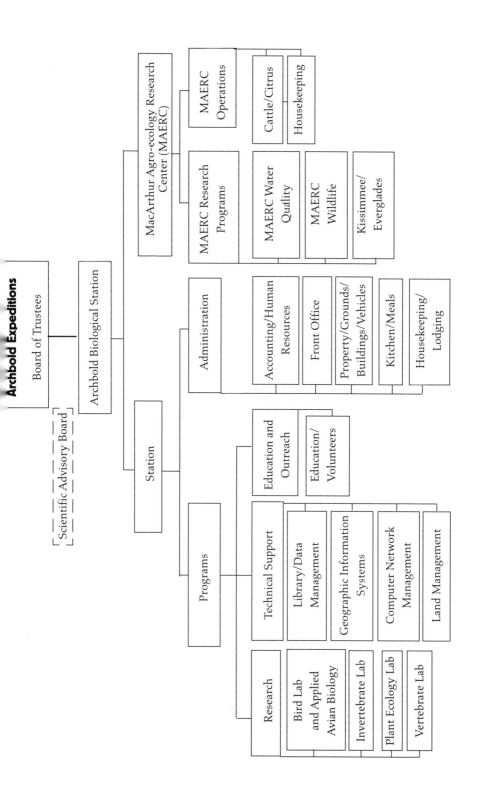

Archbold Expeditions

Board of Trustees

Scientific Advisory Board

Archbold Biological Station

MacArthur Agro-ecology Research Center (MAERC)

MAERC Research Programs
- MAERC Water Quality
- MAERC Wildlife
- Kissimmee/Everglades

MAERC Operations
- Cattle/Citrus
- Housekeeping

Station

Administration
- Accounting/Human Resources
- Front Office
- Property/Grounds/Buildings/Vehicles
- Kitchen/Meals
- Housekeeping/Lodging

Programs

Education and Outreach
- Education/Volunteers

Technical Support
- Library/Data Management
- Geographic Information Systems
- Computer Network Management
- Land Management

Research
- Bird Lab and Applied Avian Biology
- Invertebrate Lab
- Plant Ecology Lab
- Vertebrate Lab

Executive Directors, Archbold Biological Station

Name	*Term*
Richard Archbold (1907–76)	Resident director, 1941–76
James N. Layne (1926–)	June 1, 1967–December 31, 1993
James L. Wolfe (1940–)	August 1, 1985–August 1, 1988
John W. Fitzpatrick (1951–)	September 1, 1988–August 28, 1995
Hilary M. Swain (1956–)	July 31, 1995

Richard Archbold served as a research associate in the mammal department of the American Museum of Natural History from 1932 until his death.

Commemorative Stamps and Around-the-World Flight

Guba II never faltered or failed to do its duty. About the time Archbold was to return to the United States, in 1939, he was contacted by the Australians, who wanted to determine the practicality of an air route over the Indian Ocean to Europe. Archbold was glad to enter into the venture, the story of which is described in the literature published with four Cocos Island stamps as well as in three more documents discussed below. (The Cocos [Keeling] Islands are an Australian dependency in the Indian Ocean.)

The Four Cocos Island Stamps

The Cocos Island commemorative stamps, dated 1989, fifty years after the original survey flight, are (1) a forty-cent stamp with the full face of a smiling, happy, and very much in charge Captain P. G. Taylor equipped with flight headgear including goggles; (2) a seventy-cent stamp with six men standing in front of the plane and labeled "Guba II and Crew"; (3) a one-dollar stamp labeled "Guba II anchored at Direction Island," one of the several Cocos Islands; and (4) a one-dollar-and-ten-cent stamp featuring "an unissued five shilling Australian stamp." The seventy-cent stamp is especially curious. Four of the crew are dressed in single- or double-breasted business suits, neckties included, a fifth man is dressed in mechanic's coveralls, while the sixth crewman is wearing a sweatshirt. The picture is unlike any others taken of the *Guba II* crew in the South Pacific or any other picture of Richard Archbold, who, whenever he did wear a tie, always wore a bow tie.

Accounts of the Flight

It is clear from Archbold's report (1941) of the third New Guinea expedition that he did not leave the United States with the intention of flying around the world or establishing a record for doing so. However, when the opportunity occurred, Archbold did not hesitate to add this to his list of conquests. It is also clear that the Australians needed an alternate route to Europe in light of world affairs and the pending World War II. The idea of an alternate air route across the Indian Ocean was apparently that of Captain P. G. Taylor. Archbold wrote that such a trip was not too much out of their way and that a westward course would give them the advantage of the prevailing winds. The only proviso was that the Commonwealth pay for the fuel and provisions and allow Archbold to make collections en route.

At this point, it is important to place Guba's flight across the Indian Ocean—in the months of May, June, and July 1939—in the context of world events. German troops invaded Austria March 11, 1938. On March 14, 1939, Hitler called the president of Czechoslovakia to Berlin and dictated terms that allowed Germany to take what remained of that country with no opposition from any European power. On September 1, 1939, two months after Archbold landed in New York, Germany invaded Poland and World War II was under way. Australia declared war on September 3. It is no wonder that Australia was determined to find an alternate route to Europe in early 1939.

Australia's official version, taken from the literature accompanying the four stamps issued by the Cocos Islands, is that "in June 1939 the Australian Government chartered . . . [the] Guba II Flying Boat for a survey flight across the Indian Ocean with a view to ascertaining a possible alternative air route from Australia to England to use in emergency." The same literature states that the flight path was from Port Hedland in northwestern Australia, to the Cocos Islands, Diego Garcia, the Seychelles, and Kenya. No mention is made of the diversion to Jakarta (then called Batavia) due to poor weather. Accompanying the flight was Sir (later) Captain P. G. Taylor (1896–1966), decorated hero in World Wars I and II, who was "noted for his remarkable navigation accuracy." The commemorative stamp literature makes only one mention of Archbold but blatantly suggests Taylor was the pilot and in charge, whereas, in fact, he deplaned in Mombassa, the Australian interests having been satisfied, and returned home by ship. The trip across the Indian Ocean covered 4,800 nautical miles.

The Archbold version is found in a typed, unpublished, undated interview in the archives of the American Museum of Natural History and probably was made in late 1939.

Q. This Australian flight, how did that come about?

A. He [who "he" was is not explained] wrote me would I want to do it and I told them under what conditions I would. Some of the crew got extra money. They merely paid expenses.

Q. Did you ever get anything or any official recognition for that job?

A. Dinner with the Prime Minister before we left.

Q. There have been no official communications or anything along that line?

A. No but it was an official job. I expect Taylor did—the Australian.

Q. Did he actually handle the ship?

A. Just sat in the cabin.

Fortunately, Sir P. G Taylor wrote an autobiography including an interesting chapter, "Cocos, the Elusive Atoll, 1939" (Taylor 1963). Here, Taylor makes it clear that he was a navigator on this trip and that he worked closely with Lewis Yancey, for whom he obviously had a high regard, in charting their route. Taylor had searched Britain and the United States for an aircraft that could carry sufficient fuel for a long flight and was apparently surprised when he found that Archbold had the *Guba II,* the only really suitable aircraft, and that he was in New Guinea. He contacted Archbold, and they struck a deal that Taylor had no official approval to make; this approval did come later, but Taylor makes no further mention of it and we are left with Archbold's record.

In his autobiography Taylor states that "there was virtually no weather information for the route of the flight." Sure enough, the plane left Port Hedland, in the northwest corner of Australia, and soon ran into dark clouds and "torrential rain." The pilots flew high (15,000 feet) and low, to no avail. When they tried to get under the cloud cover, they found they were at 500 feet over a turbulent ocean and had very limited visibility. They searched but finally gave up and flew to Batavia, where they remained for two days waiting for the weather to clear. When they took off again, they found the Cocos with ease; they remained there for a week surveying for bases for both amphibian and land-based aircraft. The rest of the trip to Africa proved uneventful, and the mission was accomplished.

Notes

1. Herbert Lee Stoddard (1889–1968) was an outstanding ornithologist and ecologist whose career was all the more remarkable because he had only a high school education. He wrote two books (*The Bobwhite Quail* and *Memoirs of a Naturalist*) and had sixty-five articles published. From 1930 until 1943 he was director of the Cooperative Quail Study Association in Thomasville, Georgia, where he was superintendent of the Archbold estate. It was Stoddard who showed Richard Archbold and Ernst Mayr the environs of South Georgia and North Florida when the two visited there in 1931. Stoddard was a fellow of the American Ornithological Union. He finished his career as vice president of the Tall Timbers Research Station in North Florida in 1961–72.

2. Leonard C. Sanford (1868–1950) was a physician (surgeon) and self-taught ornithologist. He had a practice in New York City as well as a long association with Yale University, where he served as an instructor, surgical associate, and surgeon. He was elected to the American Museum of Natural History's board of trustees in 1921. The Leonard C. Sanford Hall of Biology of Birds was named in his honor in 1948. He gave to the museum his own collection of ten examples of every bird species found in North America north of Mexico.

Sanford had a strong influence on Richard Archbold. The men met in Europe, following Archbold's return from Madagascar, and Sanford suggested that he explore New Guinea next. Later, Sanford introduced Archbold to Ernst Mayr, suggesting that they could be of help to each other.

3. Robert T. Hatt (1902–89) served as a curator for several years at the American Museum, where his specialty was squirrels. In 1935 he became director at

the Cranbrook Institute of Science in Bloomfield Hills, Michigan, and remained in this post for the rest of his career.

4. Ernst Mayr (1904–) came to the American Museum from the Zoological Museum of the University of Berlin, where he was an assistant. He was made an honorary member of the ornithology department in 1931 for the express purpose of studying the Whitney Bird Collection from a South Seas expedition (Berger 1937). In 1933 he was named associate curator of birds, a position he held until he moved to Harvard University as director of the Agassiz Museum.

5. Kono is the local name for a rare New Guinea duck that lives on mountain lakes in the interior of the country (Berger 1937).

6. Alexander Blair (1878–1975) was a civil and structural engineer who was hired by John Roebling to oversee the construction of the roads, fences, warehouse, and other buildings on what is now the Archbold Biological Station property. Blair served as the Roeblings' representative in the purchase and construction of the fence and the first buildings at the Highlands Hammock State Park. He was later vice president of the Tropical Florida Park Association, a position he held for over thirty-five years (Wilson, unpublished). He served as president of the Florida Engineering Society and was active with several other groups (Altvater 1979). His wife was one of the early presidents of the Lake Placid Ladies Club and also active in local affairs.

7. Lake Annie was named after the wife of a local surveyor, J. W. Childs, in 1870 (Wilson, unpublished).

8. Hicoria was a town centered in the southern end of the Archbold property near the point where Old State Road 8 now crosses the railroad tracks. It included parts of sections 8, 7, and 20. The first schoolhouse in the area was built in 1920 and had about eighteen students. In 1928 a sawmill, which became operational in May 1929, was built in Hicoria. The remnants can still be found. As a result the town grew from 100 to about 1,000 people. The area lumbered stretched from south of Venus, west about twenty-five miles, and north to Sebring. At one time Hicoria was a railroad stop and had a post office and a general store. The mill closed in 1935. People drifted away, and most of the houses were moved or burned down. Only a few survived and are in use today (Wilson, unpublished).

9. Harold E. Anthony (1890–1970) began his career with the Department of Mammals and Ornithology of the American Museum of Natural History as a cataloger and general handyman in 1911 and did not obtain a curatorial ap-

pointment until 1919. In the interim he was a student at Columbia University and during World War I a captain in the artillery. He was promoted to the position of curator in 1926 and was chairman of the mammal department from 1942 to 1958, though according to a note in *The Grapevine* (anonymous 1958) he had been appointed acting head of the department in 1921 after the death of mammalogist James A. Allen. (This department had split from the Department of Ornithology in 1920). In the years 1921–42 Anthony headed the list of curators in the mammal group that appears in copies of *Natural History* magazine. Thus we assume it was Anthony with whom Archbold interacted the most during the 1930s and the New Guinea expeditions. Anthony served as president of the American Society of Mammalogists and as a director of both the New York Explorers Club and the National Audubon Society. He was also a financial expert and was active at one time as the treasurer of the New York Academy of Sciences.

10. David Fairchild (1869–1954) was with the Foreign Seed and Plant Introduction Division of the U.S. Department of Agriculture from the late 1800s until his retirement in 1928. He established the Fairchild Tropical Garden in Miami and lived in an adjacent seven-acre tropical garden known as "the Kampong." This property was purchased from his family after his death and is now a satellite garden of the Hawaiian-based National Tropical Botanical Garden. Fairchild's interests were largely utilitarian, and his association with Archbold revolved around determining how far north certain tropical and subtropical plant species might survive. His wife was an artist and a granddaughter of Alexander Graham Bell. Mrs. Fairchild worked with her husband closely. Many of his plant introductions were selected because of their food value, but he also collaborated with Thomas Edison, Henry Ford, Harvey Firestone, and others, in a search for alternate sources of latex.

11. This list was prepared by Mark Deyrup, entomologist, and Fred Lohrer, librarian and information manager at the station.

References Cited

Adkisson, C. S. 1996–97. "Aviation and the Archbold Expeditions (in four parts)." *Archbold Happenings* 2, no. 11: 15–16; 3, no. 2: 9–10; 3, no. 3: 8–9; 3, no. 4: 10–12.

Altvater, A. 1966. "Highlands Hammock." Mimeographed by the Sebring Historical Society, June 1979.

Anonymous. 1981. "Cooperative's History." *Glades Rural Electric News*. Reprinted in Bass et al. 1985.

Archbold, R. Ca. 1939. "Autobiographical Notes." Unpublished.

———. 1941. "Unknown New Guinea." *National Geographic* 79: 315–44.

Archbold, R., and A. L. Rand. 1939. *New Guinea Expedition*. New York: Robert M. McBride and Company.

Archbold, R., and G. Tate. Ca. 1940. "The Grand Valley." Unpublished.

Archbold, R., A. L. Rand, and L. J. Brass. 1948. "Results of the Archbold Expeditions, No. 41. Summary of the 1938–1939 New Guinea Expedition." *Bulletin of the American Museum of Natural History* 74: 197–288.

Bass, B. O., V. Coffey, A. Dewing, L. McNeeley, J. Roberts, N. Tatum, P. Taylor, M. Van De Velde, and E. W. Ringstaff. 1985. *Glades County, Florida, History*. Moore Haven, Fla.: Rainbow Books.

Berger, A. K. 1937. "Science in the Field and in the Laboratory." *Natural History* 37: 274.

Brass. L. J. 1944. "The Archbold Biological Station." *Science* 100: 594–95.

———. 1949. "Camps on Cape York." *Natural History* 58: 366–72.

Horner, B. E., and R. G. Van Gelder. 1979. "Obituary, Hobart Merritt Van Deusen." *Journal of Mammalogy* 60: 859–60.

Lohrer, F. Unpublished notes.

Moore, A. L. 1930. *John D. Archbold and the Early Development of Standard Oil*. New York: Macmillan.

Rand, A. L. 1936. "The Distribution and Habits of Madagascar Birds." *Bulletin of the American Museum of Natural History* 72: 143–499.

———. 1940. "Courtship of the Magnificent Bird of Paradise." *Natural History* 45: 172–75.

———. 1941. "Arizona Expedition." *Natural History* 48: 232–35.

———. 1977. Obituary, Richard Archbold. *Auk* 94: 186–87.

Rand, A. L., and L. J. Brass. 1940. "Results of the Archbold Expeditions, No. 29. Summary of the 1936–1937 New Guinea Expedition." *Bulletin of the American Museum of Natural History* 77: 341–80.

Rinald, F. A. 1948. "The Archbold Biological Station." *Natural History* 57: 226–33.

Taylor, P. G. 1963. *The Sky Beyond*. Boston: Houghton Mifflin.

Thomas, L. "Trail Blazer." 1940. *This Week Magazine,* October 27.

Van Deusen, H. M. 1966. "The Seventh Archbold Expedition." *Bioscience* 16: 449–55.

Wadlow, R. Personal communication.

Wilson, C. B. 1997. "The Brief History of Hicoria, Highlands County, Florida." Unpublished.

Yergin, D. 1993. *The Prize, the Epic Quest for Oil, Money and Power*. New York: Simon and Schuster, Touchstone Edition.

Index

Numbers in italics denote an illustration.

Roger A. Morse is professor of apiculture at Cornell University. He is the author of several hundred research and information papers and twelve books on bees and beekeeping.